Till Divorce Do Us Part

Till Divorce Do Us Part

A Practical Guide for Women in Troubled Marriages

Beverly J. Grottkau, Ph.D.

Eva Augustin Rumpf

Glenbridge Publishing Ltd.

Library of Congress Catalog Card Number: LC 95-80541

International Standard Book Number: 0-944435-39-4

Printed in the U. S. A.

To my children, Steven, Michelle, and Robert, through whom I have come to understand the true meaning of unconditional love,

To my grandchildren, through whom I have found a source of enormous joy,

To the loving memory of my mother, father, and sister, through whom I have learned that the beast residing at the center of the labyrinth is also an angel.

Beverly Grottkau

To my husband, Bill, without whose patience, support, and love neither this writing project nor our thirty-five-year marriage would have survived.

Eva Augustin Rumpf

ACKNOWLEDGMENTS

This book came to be because in both our personal and professional experiences we knew of the pain, confusion, and despair of those persons struggling with troubled marriages, agonizing over decisions about divorce, or suffering the aftereffects of marital breakup. We saw a need for solid information—whether on evaluating a relationship, understanding the legalities of divorce, helping children cope with their parents' divorce, or learning how to heal the emotional scars—particularly for those women who feel stunned and debilitated after marital rupture. We have attempted to provide this information in such a way that the lay reader as well as the professional can find help and value in it.

We are indebted to our families, friends, and colleagues who provided valuable feedback and encouragement as the project developed. We are especially grateful to Dr. Beverly Yahnke, whose vision, gentle persuasion, and constructive criticism were instrumental throughout the project; to attorneys Patricia Grove and Sandra Edhlund, whose expertise in family law provided needed direction; to Barbara Lasky, CPA, whose wisdom on financial matters was most appreciated; and to attorney Melita Biese, whose spirit and courage are reflected in a book about spirit and courage.

We also wish to thank Mary and James Keene, at Glenbridge Publishing, both of whom believed in the value of this book and who provided helpful direction, clarity, and enthusiasm, which was an important influence during the final stages of our writing.

And, finally, we wish to thank the countless men and women who have generously and courageously shared their stories and experiences with us. Collectively, they have inspired us and have brought depth and meaning to what is written in these pages. Without their willingness to share their personal struggles and triumphs, this book would lose its soul.

All names and identifying characteristics of individuals mentioned in cases and examples in this book have been changed in order to protect their privacy.

CONTENTS

INTRODUCTION

The Cleavers are gone. Ozzie and Harriet are no more. They were replaced by TV's famous single mom "Murphy Brown," the divorced men of "Misery Loves Company," and the dysfunctional family on "Married with Children." Peek into any household today and you're likely to find a single parent, a blended family, a childless couple, or unmarried partners.

Though many people may bemoan these changes and long for the family model of earlier decades, with the mother as caregiver and the father as breadwinner, only a distinct minority of America's population fits this family profile. The only vestige of the so-called "traditional" family that may live on is the nostalgia experienced by some older Americans for that which was once defined as a standard for family life. Indeed, any attempt to define the "typical" or "ideal" family of today is an exercise in futility.

Many societal transformations have precipitated the demise of what historians have dubbed the "nuclear family"—a family that focused on the procreation of children and consisted of a lifelong, sexually exclusive, heterosexual, monogamous marriage in which the female was a full-time housewife and the male was the primary provider. The waning of this model has been attributed to a variety of social trends, including a decline in the birth rate, the sexual revolution, and the acceleration of women into the labor force.

But surely, the divorce revolution that has taken place since the 1960s ranks as one of the key factors that has transformed family structure, functions, and norms in contemporary society. Today, one of every two recorded marriages ends in divorce. Add to this statistic the number of unrecorded desertions, separations, and breakups of "living-together-but-not-married" arrangements (for which accurate figures are hard to come by), and we have a startling picture of the disruption and fragmentation of today's families.

The divorce revolution has given birth to a whole new vocabulary, as men, women, and even children cope with the changes and traumas of divorce. Becoming familiar terms in many households are words such as: mediation, temporary restraining order, mandatory arrest, physical placement, legal and joint custody, child support, maintenance, and—reflecting the loss of confidence in marital permanence—prenuptial agreement.

As the prevalence of divorce continues to transform society, the split family may one day become the norm. If divorce becomes as common as marital permanence, men and women who marry may engage in behaviors and ways of thinking that generate a self-fulfilling prophecy that leads to the eventual breakdown of their marriage.

This book has been written to meet the needs of women in troubled marriages who are not prepared to face the threat of divorce. We will explore those personal, legal, and financial factors that must be addressed by women in order for them to: (a) assess the nature of their relationships and carefully weigh the option of divorce; (b) reduce the harmful psychological effects of loss that divorcing women experience; (c) increase the potential for their fair and equal treatment in the courts; and, (d) find those resources that can enhance their personal and professional lives as they adjust to living as uncoupled individuals.

In addition, since most children remain with their mothers following divorce, this book is intended to assist mothers in developing effective strategies to diminish the psychological trauma children experience as they attempt to adjust to loss and to accommodate to a new and unfamiliar family structure.

Our goal in writing this book is to increase the potential for positive outcomes for women as they negotiate the many facets of loss through separation and divorce, and to empower women, either as parents or single adults, as they attempt to reach their fullest potential. A feeling of empowerment, which enables one to make responsible choices, is the opposite of the intense feelings of helplessness and hopelessness that many women experience following separation and divorce. A woman undergoing divorce may feel "out of control" and say: "I'm not okay . . . the world is a hostile place . . . I am unable to do anything to make things better."

The woman who is able to develop a measure of internal strength and power over her predicament will likely gain a sense of control over her perceived helplessness and hopelessness. This empowerment is not equated with a "claw-your-way-to-the-top-without-breaking-your-fingernails" scenario. Rather than learning aggression, dominance, control, oppression, and autocratic behavior, women who feel helpless need to develop a humane sense of assertive power that will foster self-efficacy, capacity, and accomplishment. It is the premise of this book that this process can be enhanced through access to information and a variety of resources.

The decade of the 1970s is recalled as a time when women began to look inward in order to define new ways to nourish their unmet needs. After years of believing our "rightful" place was in the home, many of us began to experience a sense of restlessness and started to rethink the prescribed role that society had imposed upon us. In our searching we also began to ponder existential questions such as, "Who am I?" "What do I want," and "What's in it for me?" These ruminations had a profound effect on women of the '70s, and the road ahead was paved with change and new opportunities.

The journey, however, was not without its roadblocks. Working women, for example, recognized that, while new options gave them access to roles previously assigned only to middle-class, white men, a wall of tradition and stereotypes prevented them from reaching their highest potential and created a barrier to advancement. In their book, *Breaking the Glass Ceiling*, Ann Morrison and her colleagues at the Center for Creative Leadership created the perfect metaphor to visualize the predicament of women who attempt to advance in an organization. These women, noted Morrison, eventually reach a "glass ceiling," an invisible barrier that keeps them from reaching higher levels simply because they are women.[1]

Many women attempted to break through the barrier by working harder and longer, and, not coincidentally, the "superwoman" and "supermom" syndromes emerged. For many married women, who also served as primary caretakers in their dual-career families, the advice of their male counterparts, "Don't work harder, work smarter," was met with disgust. They realized they already were working as "smart" as they could, given their multiple responsibilities as wives, caretakers, and workers.

Then, during the latter part of the 1980s, articles in professional journals and popular magazines began to throw darts at the "Superwoman Syndrome," attacking it as a myth. The truth, these articles said, was that many women didn't want to have it all, and that those who did want it all could not have it without paying an enormous price. One of the prices, women learned, was that men were beginning to have trouble relating to them. In addition, many women began to discover that their husbands were feeling intimidated as the wives developed new careers, returned to school, and no longer fit the traditional mold of the wife and mother their husbands and children once knew and relied upon.

As Harriet Lerner points out in her book *Dance of Anger*, when a woman begins to make clear statements about her needs, wants, beliefs, and priorities, her husband may feel significantly threatened and plead for or demand the return of the previous status. If the woman gives up under the pressure and resumes her earlier pattern of functioning, the sacrifices to her self-concept and self-esteem could lead to the repression of anger and ultimately to depression.[2]

On the other hand, if she chooses not to compromise her self-esteem and continues to pursue a new level of assertiveness, autonomy, and maturity, the resulting anxieties and uncertainties experienced by her husband could create the catalyst for marital discontent and eventual breakdown. As divorce became another price to pay, women in these situations learned that striking a healthy balance between individualism and togetherness was a serious and tricky business.

As women redefined their options and assumed new roles outside the home, those who divorced began to realize that, though their professional needs were being met, some of their emotional needs were not. Particularly for the traditional woman, who had defined herself as wife and mother, her needs to nurture and be nurtured were being sacrificed.

This phenomenon was illustrated dramatically after a presentation by one of the authors to a large group of higher education teachers, administrators, and adult returning students. She had pointed out that as women stretch to reach new heights professionally, many appear to be paying the price with unfulfilled intimacy and belongingness needs. Following her presentation, a number of women rushed up to her to enthusiastically agree with her observation. Some of the women reported that what they missed most in their newly discovered autonomy was "being taken care of"! The speaker had struck a nerve.

For some women, independence has resulted in a form of social isolation and an absence of intimate relationships. Hence, it appears that the independence ushered in by the tide of new opportunities in the 1970s and the decades that followed also became the catalyst for a new form of unmet needs. In this sense, the 1970s—a decade that held promise for countless numbers of American women—ironically set the stage for yet a new form of existential emptiness. Within such a milieu, it is not so remarkable that women, who may be competent professionally, are frequently unable to engage in meaningful intimate relationships. What's more, they often are unaware of ways in which they might comfort, nourish, and soothe themselves.

This book is couched in the belief that unless women learn new ways of behaving, and unless they are able to discover who they really are and what they truly want (as opposed to who they "should" be and what they think they need, which typically was provided by a man), they will continue to hold the short end of the psychological stick. Conversely, the woman who is able to discover a genuine sense of self is more likely to develop an integrated wholeness and a healthy sense of independence that can become the precursor to an interdependent, intimate relationship.

It is against this tapestry of changing conditions and associated psychological and situational conflicts that we wrote this book as a practical guide for women who may be in varying stages of separation and divorce. The following should be underscored:

a) This book does not advocate divorce. As will be shown, there are ways of assessing whether there is hope for the couple in a troubled marriage and what might be done if they have not already made the decision to divorce. (b) The book is not intended to provide solutions, but rather to serve as a tool to facilitate the process of restructuring the many facets of a woman's life, based on where she is on the separation/divorce continuum. In this sense, the book can be a measuring stick to assess where she is at a given time, and it provides options that might be available to her at that point in the process. (c) The book must be read as one resource, and readers should keep in mind that, as situational and psychological dilemmas surface, professional help may be needed for support and advice if problems persist.

The case studies and illustrations used in this book are drawn from the experiences of real individuals and/or are based on themes that are central in women's lives. The ideas, procedures, and suggestions are not intended as substitutes for consulting with your physician or a mental health professional. Matters regarding your emotional and physical well-being may require medical supervision.

1

THE MARRIAGE THAT'S FALLING APART: IS DIVORCE INEVITABLE?

The man and woman sat in the therapist's office, anxious and fearful that problems were destroying their twenty-year marriage. They had sought counseling in the hope that somehow they could salvage their relationship and avoid the road to divorce court.

The therapist turned to the wife and posed the question: "If, when you awake tomorrow morning, something would change that would let you know your husband really cares about you, what would that be?"

The wife responded almost immediately: "Once in a while he would send me flowers at my workplace to show he thinks about me and values me."

The husband, looking stunned, replied: "Why didn't you ever tell me?"

She answered: "I thought, if you cared, you would have known."

"Till death do us part."

The traditional marriage vow, uttered by countless couples through the ages, was a commitment to permanence. Unable to

8

see what the future held beyond their wedding day, they nevertheless pledged to face it together. They knew, or would soon learn, that healthy marriages rarely just happen. The relationship would require work, patience, courage, flexibility, and communication as the partners went through a series of inevitable changes over time in their growth and development.

Today, a "till-divorce-do-us-part" attitude appears to more accurately characterize the way in which many couples enter marriage. Rather than an assumption of permanence, an image of tentativeness about marital relationships seems to be more common. Whether they acknowledge it or not, couples know that today's revolving door approach to marriage sanctions a way out if things turn sour.

This attitude is reflected in the now common greeting of old friends who haven't seen each other for years: "Are you still married?" The expectation is that the divorce epidemic has struck again. The answer that elicits surprise—even amazement—is, "Yes, we're still married."

The practice of divorce law, with all its attending drama and cast of characters, spawned its own television series in the early '90s. It took only a few decades for "Civil Wars"—the weekly drama about three divorce lawyers—to replace "Father Knows Best," that icon of the 1950s.

It appears that marriage has become another castoff in America's throwaway society, along with disposable cameras, razors, contact lenses, watches, diapers, and sterile needles. While divorce was unthinkable for most people in previous generations, it has now become an acceptable and readily available alternative once a relationship has been "used up."

In the heat of marital strife, the lure of greener grass elsewhere often causes a partner to bolt. How much easier it seems to leave problems behind than to work on solving them! Yet, for those who commit themselves to learning new ways to create a healthier bond, the pain of divorce can be avoided.

Even in very troubled marriages, divorce is not necessarily inevitable. The case that follows illustrates a number of problems that surface when a relationship begins to disintegrate. The discussion that follows the case study suggests several techniques that can be used both to assess a threatened relationship and to minimize the potential for breakup and loss.

JOAN AND BEN: A TROUBLED MARRIAGE

Joan and Ben knew their marriage was in serious trouble, but they weren't sure why. Each felt the other no longer wanted to be in the relationship, yet both said they were committed to the marriage. They no longer knew how to communicate effectively with each other, and each had retreated into an isolated, self-protective world. The pair had been married for just under ten years, but, because they were so disconnected and had spent so little time enriching their marriage, they had lost the bonding seen in healthy relationships. Instead, they resembled two shy, anxious, immature teenagers.

Joan, a homemaker, cared for their two children because she felt she was expected to. She had dinner on the table at the same time every night, kept their home immaculate, and rarely took time out for herself. Her days were filled with thoughts about how unhappy she was with the sameness of her life. She was feeling trapped but didn't know what she really wanted.

Ben felt certain about his masculine role in the family and based his notions about division of labor in the home on traditional gender roles. He saw himself as the wage earner and decision-maker in the family and felt his wife should remain at home with their children while they were young. Ben traced the breakdown in communication with Joan to the time when the children were born. He looked forward to the day when they were grown and out of the nest so, as he put it, he could have his "old wife back."

Joan and Ben rarely argued. In fact, they rarely talked. They said they had tried to resolve differences in the past but never seemed to get anywhere. Ben would yell, and Joan, feeling victimized and unloved, would retreat to the bedroom. Days would go by with neither speaking to the other and each feeling powerless, hopeless, and frustrated.

Ben and Joan's finances were in a shambles, and their sex life was a disaster. Their young children, sensing the disintegration of the family, were becoming demanding, strong-willed, and uncooperative. The couple began avoiding family and friends, who felt uncomfortable around Ben and Joan and offered unwelcomed advice.

REACHING FOR HELP

Joan and Ben decided to seek counseling because they were unable to talk with each other about what they saw as the impending destruction of their marriage. The emotional pain they were experiencing almost daily created a state of readiness that made them open to the help they could find in therapy.

When couples in conflict see a counselor, they typically describe their dilemma as a communications problem. Their attempts at communication usually revolve around practical concerns like children or finances. Despite numerous attempts to resolve the issues, nothing seems to work. Discussions deadlock or explode into angry confrontations.

The role of the therapist is to help the couple identify the strategies they have used in the past—both those that worked at one time and those that don't work. Looking at strategies that have worked before shows the couple that they already have developed some effective skills they can use again. Identifying strategies that don't work can point the way to more effective alternatives. In other words, this process can help the couple put into practice the principles that "If it works, don't fix it," and "If it's not working, do something different."

When both you and your spouse seek counseling, you are conveying the message that each of you is concerned about the direction the marriage has taken and that each wants to do something about it. However, the mere appearance of both spouses at the counselor's office is not a guarantee that each individual is seriously committed to working for change.

One partner may show up at the session in order to ensure that his/her image and reputation are not damaged. The individual who appears only for the purpose of monitoring the sessions is considered a visitor. In this case, the therapist tries to help the visitor become a customer—one who buys into the idea that the marriage will be more satisfying if both partners learn new ways of handling conflict. The couple must recognize that conflict doesn't thrive in a vacuum but is the outgrowth of an unhealthy response of two people to a situation.

When a woman pursues therapy as an individual, her growth and development over time can have either a positive or negative effect on the spouse who is not in treatment. As she changes and exhibits healthier behavior, her husband—familiar with the old, dysfunctional patterns—may feel confused and threatened. If he was more comfortable with his former, though less healthy, wife, he may want her back.

On the other hand, a woman in therapy can have a positive influence on her spouse who is not in treatment, although this may take much time and persistence. The challenge to the woman is that she not succumb to the predictable but subtle nudges around her—which may come from her children and extended family—that she return to her old ways of behaving.

THE BLAME GAME

People who are having marital difficulties, such as those illustrated in the case of Joan and Ben, often vent their built-up frustrations by engaging in a blame game. Because they feel out of control, they use blame to achieve a sense of power over their partners as well as over the predicament in which they find themselves.

Unfortunately, this false sense of power prevents us from looking honestly at ourselves and impedes our ability to more clearly understand the role we may have played in the marriage's problems. Playing the blame game restricts our capacity for letting go of the resentment we harbor.

People often have great difficulty moving beyond such a "pity party" mentality. By feeling victimized we don't have to work at changing anything. Neither do we have to subject ourselves to feelings of discomfort and potential rejection. However, by learning new ways to more assertively express who we are and what we want, we can develop a healthier self-concept. This, in turn, can increase our chance of discovering a more fulfilling relationship with our partner.

THE "SHOULD SYNDROME"

Like Joan and Ben, many couples also suffer from the "should syndrome." Their choices and their behavior are governed by compliance with the expectations of society, which are usually based on stereotypic, gender-role models. Couples who believe they *should* behave in certain ways are driven by a need to fulfill these externally imposed expectations and sanctions.

The "shoulds," which promote conformity and may have no rational basis, are often deep-rooted ones learned in childhood. Adults often blindly comply with these rules and standards, never questioning their value and usefulness. "Shoulds" have an almost mystical power over us, and they can lock us into behavior patterns that resist change. The more we follow expectations for what we should be or should do, the less able we are to bring about positive change in our lives.

The old "should tapes" that play in our heads often create anxiety and foster irrational thinking. We may believe that if we don't meet expectations, something catastrophic will happen. For example, a mother might say, "I should be at home with my children, and it would be absolutely disastrous for them if I ever had to be employed outside the home."

If we feel compelled to comply with the "shoulds" of life, it can be helpful to look at our unexamined, mythical belief systems and question those perceptions that can create negative emotional consequences for us. When we challenge this unnecessary external clutter, we free ourselves to attend to the quality of our internal life, both as individuals and as partners in a loving relationship.

In Joan's case, her irrational belief system led her to try to be a perfect mother and wife, devoting her life to her family's well-being and happiness. She felt she never quite measured up to these standards of perfection, but she didn't talk about the feelings of anxiety this internal struggle created. Joan believed she was expected to play the hand of cards she had been dealt. She couldn't imagine folding the hand and dealing herself a new one. She felt helpless and hopeless.

Joan's feelings of helplessness generated a great deal of anger. But because she had learned early in life that females should be able to control their anger, she had nowhere to go with her emotions. Typically, Joan turned her anger inward. The stage was set for a serious case of clinical depression.

Ben, of course, had his own "shoulds." He had learned the expected male roles early in life. Counseling helped Joan and Ben to see that they were "shoulding all over themselves." They learned to recognize the external forces that were controlling their lives, including the expectations of family, friends, and Ben's job. They began to question these externally imposed expectations and to look inward at their personal wants and needs. In short, they replaced their "shoulds" with "coulds."

When we begin to express our desires, we often feel guilty doing so. But as we begin to feel more comfortable talking about our wants and needs, we develop an "I'm OK, you're OK" attitude, which fosters a sense of acceptance and diminished feelings of selfishness. We are then able to identify some "coulds" as reasonable and desirable options for ourselves.

In addition, as we learn to communicate our needs to our partners, we can overcome feelings of rejection when our spouse is unable to provide what is being asked for. Women who communicate their needs also realize that suffering in silence is a passive, unhealthy response that only fuels the fire of their anger.

Counseling helped Joan to acknowledge the sense of shame and humiliation she had carried inside because she saw herself as a failure, unable to attain her own personal goals, or to succeed as a partner in intimacy with her husband. Before she sought help, Joan's response to her situation was the desire to get rid of those factors in her life that she felt were creating her conflict, namely her husband and children. These feelings only added to her burden of guilt and shame.

As Joan acknowledged her complex and often conflicting feelings and learned to assertively express her wants and needs, her anger steadily diminished and her depressive symptoms gradually began to subside.

THE DUAL IMAGE MARRIAGE

It's probably safe to say that no two partners view their marriage in exactly the same way. Not only do individuals perceive the relationship from different perspectives, but a woman's picture of her spouse is likely to be very different from how he sees himself. Such dual images can create different expectations and become the source of marital discord.

Partners' differences in perceptions of marriage and each other can be gauged by using the Marital Assessment instrument (see Table 1). The assessment tool is based on the work of Edward Waring, a therapist who has studied the major intimacy factors of couples experiencing marital discord.[1]

Questions 1 through 7 help the couple become aware of how each views the relationship. Question 8, the "miracle question," gives the couple an opportunity to disclose what each wants from the relationship. The request is stated in concrete, behavioral terms so the other person knows exactly what is being asked for.

For example, in response to the question, "What would be different?" the answer, "He would be nicer to me," is not acceptable, since "nice" means different things to different people. On the other hand, statements like "He would do the dishes twice a week" increase the likelihood that the spouse will be able to comply.

The "miracle question" is important for several reasons. It may provide the first opportunity for the partner to let his or her needs be known. Furthermore, answers to this question help define solutions to problems in the marriage.

Finally, behaviors that are requested by partners and subsequently responded to by their spouses can begin a healthy cycle of change in a troubled marriage. Those changes can have a dramatic effect on the psyche of both men and women as they begin to feel they are being taken seriously.

What's more, it appears that attempts by a spouse to change are every bit as important as the precision with which the requested behavior is being carried out. When a man begins to respond to his partner's needs, the message to the woman is, "He really is trying; therefore, he must really care." However, there are some men who miss the whole point of trying:

> Men have great difficulty seeing the connection between expressing their love and picking up their socks. But that is exactly the point: one test of true love is whether each of you is willing, without reservation and with no

expectation of anything in return, to respond to the other's values. When you love and respect someone, you realize that what is trivial to you may be important to her, and therefore you make it important to you, too.[2]

The relationship factors, which are outlined in the Marital Assessment instrument, provide an operational way of defining intimacy. If we exhibit these factors to a high degree, we are likely to have a deeper level of healthy intimacy in our relationship.

When we compare with our partner our ratings on the ten-point scale for each of the factors, we can recognize where our strengths and weaknesses lie—as perceived by ourselves and by our partner. Partners can then ask one another what would have to change in order for the score to move up one point on each factor.

When you request behavioral change from your partner in concrete terms, it allows him to say how much of what is being asked for can willingly be given at that point without compromising his values. If too much compromise is required, values can be clarified and resolution reached by using the conflict resolution strategy discussed later in this chapter.

Tools such as the Marital Assessment instrument can be an important first step in helping us learn about ourselves and what we consider important and meaningful in our relationship.

BEYOND INTIMACY

Intimacy can be defined in many ways, and the meaning we subscribe to may be a function of our age as well as the developmental stage in which we find ourselves. The relationship factors we discussed previously offer us one way of measuring the many facets of intimacy.

While intimacy is an important ingredient of loving relationships, it appears to be but one of several components of mature love. Yale professor Robert Sternberg suggests that not

---

TABLE 1

Marital Assessment

1. How are feelings expressed between you and your spouse?

2. How is behavior change requested? Maintained?

3. What are the strengths of your current relationship? Weaknesses?

4. What attracted you to each other?

5. What are your theories about why current problems exist?

6. How was conflict handled early during your relationship?

7. At what point in your present relationship did each perceive dissatisfaction?

8. If, as you sleep tonight, a miracle would happen, and when you wake in the morning, your relationship would be healthier, what would be different?

Relationship Factors (adapted from Waring, 1988): rate each factor on a scale of 1 to 10 (1 = low degree; 10 = high degree):

☐   a.) Conflict Resolution: The ease with which differences of opinion are resolved.

☐ b.) Affection: The degree to which feelings of emotional closeness are expressed by the couple.

☐ c.) Cohesion: The degree to which the couple is committed to the marriage.

☐ d.) Sexuality: The degree to which sexual needs are communicated and fulfilled by the marriage.

☐ e.) Identity: The couple's level of self-confidence and self-esteem.

☐ f.) Compatibility: The degree to which the couple is able to work and play together comfortably.

☐ g.) Autonomy: The success with which the couple has gained independence from their families of origin and their offspring.

☐ h.) Expressiveness: The degree to which thoughts, beliefs, attitudes and feelings are shared within the marriage.

Review carefully your ratings of each of the above eight factors and determine what you would personally want to change in order to choose to move up one point on each factor that shows a low rating.

Now compare your ratings with your spouse's. Are you surprised by any of your partner's responses? Are there any factors which show a large discrepancy between your rating and your spouse's? What change would you request from your spouse in order to facilitate movement upward in an area that you feel needs improvement? How would you request the change? Is the change being requested capable of being observed so that each of you will know that an attempt has been made?

only intimacy (the feeling of closeness, connectedness and bond-edness), but also passion (the drives that lead to physical attrac-tion, romance, and sexual consummation) and commitment (the decision that a person loves another and wants to maintain that love) are separate and essential components found in loving rela-tionships.[3]

The depth of a loving relationship appears to depend upon the amount of all three components that two people share as part-ners. Furthermore, the way in which two people define the type of relationship they share depends upon the strength of each of the components relative to each other. For example, when a rela-tionship consists primarily of passion, a partner may say, "We have a lot of good sex, but there isn't much of anything else." Similarly, if intimacy based on a sense of connectedness is para-mount, a partner might complain, "I feel like I'm living with a roommate."

On the other hand, a relationship that is committed but lacks intimacy and passion may simply be grounded in obliga-tion or convenience, leading a partner to say, "I could never leave my husband while my children are young," or, "We live like strangers, but we stay together for economic and social reasons." Such a commitment based on factors external to the couple becomes very restrictive to the growth and development of a loving relationship. Unless the couple can recognize the dif-ference between being committed to a partner and being commit-ted to the institution of marriage, a divorce is likely when the situation changes and the glue of obligation or convenience no longer holds the family together.

If we and our partners are willing to take the risk of dis-cussing our perceptions of the strength of intimacy, passion, and commitment in our relationship, we have an excellent chance of ridding ourselves of old, habitual, and restrictive ways of defin-ing it. We are then free to develop a new, more mature loving relationship.

Taking risks is often essential to growth. As the lobster grows, it must rid itself of its old, restrictive shell or it will die. However, between the shedding of the old shell and the generation of the new, the lobster renders itself vulnerable. So it is in relationships that are going through a growth process, and the need for sensitivity and compassion for each other as the change occurs is imperative.

THE POROUS ROCK

The case of Joan and Ben illustrates another problem many women in our society still experience: Joan was unable to define her identity as a person apart from the significant others in her life. When Joan's counselor asked her, "Who are you?" she responded, "I am Ben's wife," and "I am Ann and Rick's mother."

A woman who feels her rightful place is in the home is often unable to define herself apart from the roles she plays there. She passively accepts a view of herself that others created and imposed on her, and she does nothing to change this condition. Self-definition that is absorbed from the outside, rather than created within oneself, can cause anxiety about the meaning and purpose of one's life.

An identity problem of this nature isn't confined to women who are housewives and mothers. Women who work outside the home and are married to successful men may center their lives on their husbands and find their identity through them. Should the husbands of these women leave them or die, the women predictably feel vulnerable and rudderless. Their limited ego strength can plunge them into serious clinical depression.

Like Joan, women who define themselves through others speak of having no substance and feeling empty. When they look within, some see only a black hole. One woman graphically described herself as a transparent amoeba, quietly going about the business of finding material in the external world to attach herself to.

Women who experience such intense feelings of emptiness can be compared to a porous volcanic rock that lies passively on the seashore, waiting to be filled. While it may appear beautiful and sturdy from a distance, closer inspection shows it is covered with holes that collect water and debris washed up from the ocean. Old water runs out; new material is carried in. The content of the rock is ever changing.

Like the porous rock, women who feel empty often fill the void by living vicariously through their children or spouses. They soak up the opinions, thoughts, and behaviors of others. They become actors on life's stage, taking their roles from movies they've seen and novels they've read. Some try to fill the void with food or alcohol. Unfortunately, this process of absorbing the substitutes of the external world can restrict a woman's capacity to make healthy personal choices. The choices she does make may be detrimental to her physical and mental health.

To break the porous rock syndrome, we must be willing to take a serious, honest look at our lives. We must recognize the blueprint we were born with—our genetic predispositions—as well as the life script we learned from family and society. As one person observed, "The goal of therapy is to see how much of the blueprint and life script we want to change as free-choosing, responsible adults, so that we can become more of what we are and less of what we are expected to be."

RESOLVING CONFLICTS

"Opposites attract," the old saying goes. Indeed, we frequently, and quite unconsciously, look to others to complement those deficiencies we see in ourselves. A shy individual may marry a gregarious person, or a dreamer may choose a pragmatic partner. During courtship and early marriage, these differences seem to cause minimal damage. When the couple is still in the romantic stage of the relationship, they are more likely to defer to the other.

Inevitably, as the marriage progresses, the veneer of acceptance of differences begins to break down. When the communication gap becomes vast, we begin the disengagement process. Loving diminishes when partners are unable or unwilling to understand, respect, appreciate, and accept their differences.

Responses like these begin to emerge with more frequency: "You know I hate football; you go by yourself," or "Why do you always want to see love stories when you know I like war movies?" The differences between the partners are accentuated and become a source of conflict.

Furthermore, while we can usually defer more patiently to one another's differences *when things are going well,* this deference may give way to fury when a marriage is experiencing conflict. The partner's opposite qualities that attracted and intrigued us at first can become fodder for marital breakdown.

During confrontation, other differences, perhaps not apparent earlier, begin to emerge, such as differences in the way people process information and resolve conflict. The couple soon realizes that what worked at an earlier time in their marriage is no longer effective. The harsh reality hits; the honeymoon is truly over.

Such a crisis provides an opportunity for us to learn new ways to handle conflict. Each partner needs to take responsibility for the role he or she has played in the conflict. And each must learn to exercise a healthy assertiveness, which is the ability to actively communicate how one feels and thinks in a way that does not violate the rights of others. This means abandoning tactics like commanding, demanding, ordering, and blaming. Only then can we resolve problems in a direct, nonmanipulative manner that does not shut down communication.

Some couples, like Joan and Ben, seldom engage in any communication at all. Their inability to confront and settle conflict prevents differences from ever being resolved. They walk away, leaving the issues to fester. They need to learn how to face their differences and use conflict resolution skills, which are not difficult, but take practice.

The systematic conflict resolution strategy, illustrated in Table 2, is an adaptation of a problem-solving flow chart devised by I.D. Turkat and J.F. Calhoun.[4] Individuals may use portions of the strategy without being aware they are doing so. But the potential for successful conflict resolution can be increased if we use a systematic process, which provides feedback about where we are at any given point in the conflict.

Using this systematic approach helps a couple to determine who owns the problem by asking the question, "With whose life is the conflict interfering?" For example, if the problem exists for your spouse, you simply need to be empathic and show awareness of how he might be feeling and why. This response keeps you from becoming enmeshed in his problem, yet it provides healthy support without interference and imposition.

On the other hand, when a problem affects your own life, you must convey to your spouse what he is doing, how you feel about it, and why. This is employing healthy assertiveness. The remaining steps to the conflict resolution strategy are outlined in Table 2 and are simple to implement.

As couples begin to systematically use their conflict resolution skills, new alternatives can open up for them to find acceptable options for addressing their problems. The strategy can also be taught to children so they can learn to resolve their own conflicts at home and at school, thereby building self-empowerment and inner directedness.

TAKING TIME FOR EACH OTHER

Joan and Ben were typical of many married people whose lives have become filled with such duties as parenting, working, keeping house, paying bills, and so on. Their attention had become

TABLE 2

Conflict Resolution Skills

1. Decide who owns the problem.

   a. If the other person owns the problem, an empathic response would include:

   You feel _____ , because _____ .

   b. If you own the problem, the message would include:

   When you _____ , I feel _____ , because _____.

2. Concretely state the problem together. Break the problem down to its smallest part and ensure that each of you understands and agrees on the nature of the problem.

3. Write down on a piece of paper possible alternatives that could help you resolve the problem. Even if the alternative seems silly, put it down, because it may generate other more appropriate options. (Note: When only one individual owns the problem, that person is required to generate ALL alternatives in order to emphasize a sense of individual ownership. When BOTH partners own the problem, however, in order to stress a sense of mutual ownership, the couple is expected to alternate responses until all options are exhausted.)

4. Eliminate any alternative that is an obviously inappropriate choice.

5. Examine each alternative one at a time. List the advantages of choosing that alternative. Then list the disadvantages of choosing the same alternative. (Again, if BOTH partners own the problem, the couple should alternate listing these advantages and disadvantages until all possible negative and positive consequences are exhausted.)

6. Eliminate any alternative if it generates mostly negative consequences.

7. Select the most positive alternative. (If BOTH partners own the problem, it is essential that there is mutual agreement on the chosen alternative.)

8. Generate a list, using steps 3 through 6, of all possible strategies that might be used to implement the selected alternative, i.e., "What will it take to implement this option?"

9. Select and implement the most positive strategy to resolve the conflict.

10. Re-evaluate at a predetermined date the effectiveness of the selected alternative in resolving the conflict.

11. If the conflict persists, choose a new alternative from the list of original alternatives, or, based on new information about the problem, develop a new list of alternatives and strategies using steps 3 through 10.

Adapted from "The Problem-Solving Flow Chart," by I.D. Turkat and J.F. Calhoun, 1980, *The Behavior Therapist*, v. 3, no. 3, p. 21. Copyright 1980 by the Association for the Advancement of Behavior Therapy. Reprinted by permission of the publisher and the author.

focused away from their personal needs and toward external tasks. Predictably, their marriage suffered from boredom and monotony. They spent little time with each other, and the mere thought of doing so provoked anxiety for each of them.

It is not uncommon for couples who, after years of raising children, face the empty nest—and the thought of being alone together—with a sense of trepidation. They may never have learned to relate to each other on more than a task-oriented basis. Such a situation can lead to marital rupture. Spending time together can revive the mutual emotional involvement that once characterized a couple's relationship.

For example, you and your partner could resolve to spend one night a week together, for at least two hours, in a public place. A public place is suggested as a way to avoid the many distractions at home, which are often the source of the conflicts that plague couples. It's not easy to overlook the tasks that need to be accomplished, the ringing phone, the bickering children, the unpaid bills. Furthermore, in the public eye, couples are less likely to argue or to walk away.

When you schedule the same evening every week for each other, you come to depend on this time together. It's recommended that you not participate in anything at this time that would direct your attention away from each other, such as a movie, concert, or spectator sport. An important side effect of the weekly arrangement is the message it conveys to the couples, their family, and their friends that nothing takes precedence over their time together. And while couples may initially find it difficult to communicate with each other for two hours, dialogue should become easier as the weeks pass and they begin to look forward to their special time together.

An important by-product of spending time together is the change in perception that children develop toward their parents. When parents are perceived as unified, children no longer are able to divide their loyalties between parents. Furthermore, as a couple becomes a more cohesive unit, children who at one time may have been the center of their parents' attention are no longer the pampered recipients of misdirected love. In order to feel genuinely secure, children do not need overindulgence but a healthy form of love that includes consistent, clearly defined expectations and discipline. And as couples learn to refocus their attention toward each other, their children become less demanding, manipulative, and contrary.

We began this chapter with the premise that not every troubled marriage is destined to end in divorce court. We discussed a few of the many strategies that can help a couple revitalize their marriage so that divorce is not inevitable. It is important to point out that while the strategies we have described may be successful and sufficient for some couples, for others they may be just a starting point.

It is crucial to recognize that the strategies that have been suggested will be successful only to the extent that both partners are committed to change. If couples care enough to try, they may discover that some vestige of the love that brought them together years ago lies dormant beneath their hurt and anger and disappointment.

No one can make another person change, any more than we can make a person love us or want to be married to us. In some troubled marriages, a point is reached when one or both partners know the covenant of trust, love, and respect has been irreparably damaged. When that point of no return is reached, there is a sense that one can no longer turn back, and the predictable stages of marital dissolution are set in motion.

Chapter Two discusses those stages that will likely occur when a couple, for whatever reason, is unable to resolve the cumulative conflicts that have fractured their marriage. Understanding these stages can help women (and men as well) feel a greater sense of control over their predicament as they attempt to negotiate the early warning signs of marital disintegration.

CHECKLIST

Below are 16 statements to help you detect the extent to which your marriage is suffering from some of the problems discussed in Chapter One. This checklist is designed to be used only as a guide and can serve to increase your knowledge about yourself and your marriage.

Directions: Read each statement carefully and, using the following key, indicate to the left how true it is for you.

1 = Not at all true
2 = Somewhat true
3 = Moderately true
4 = Considerably true
5 = Extremely true

☐ 1. When I am angry, I keep my feelings to myself.

☐ 2. It is difficult to express freely my wants and needs to my spouse.

☐ 3. Sometimes I would like to do things without my spouse, such as go to a movie with a woman friend, but I don't think he would understand.

☐ 4. When my spouse and I disagree, we are unable to openly discuss our conflict.

☐ 5. My spouse and I are unable to resolve most everyday problems.

☐   6. When my spouse and I communicate, we talk about practical matters, such as family finances and child rearing, and rarely spend time discussing our relationship needs.

☐   7. I blame others for the terrible condition my marriage is in.

☐   8. I don't know who I am or what I want.

☐   9. I have difficulty living up to others' expectations of me.

☐ 10. I feel like a miserable failure.

☐ 11. My spouse and I are very different, and we have not learned to understand and respect these differences.

☐ 12. My spouse and I rarely take time out to have fun together.

☐ 13. I wish there were more excitement in my marriage.

☐ 14. My marriage is in serious trouble.

☐ 15. My spouse and I are not doing all we can to help our relationship succeed.

☐ 16. I believe my spouse and I could benefit from marital counseling.

Responses with high ratings (4 – considerably true, 5 – extremely true) can serve as a beginning point for meaningful discussions with your spouse about ways to improve your relationship. For example, if you have a rating of 5 for statement number 12, you might talk with your spouse about what it would take to have more fun together.

Without the skill of a counselor, you may not know why you feel the way you do, think the way you do, or behave the way you do. Therefore, as you discuss the checklist with your spouse, focus positively on the how's, what's, where's, and when's and not the why's. For example, don't ask, "Why aren't we having fun together?" Rather, ask, "How might we have more fun together; what specifically might we do; where and when might we do it?"

This checklist can also serve as a useful tool for recognizing different points of view between partners. By asking your spouse to complete the checklist for himself and comparing your answers, you can begin to understand more clearly the differences and similarities in how you see yourselves and your marriage relationship.

2

SO YOU ARE
CONTEMPLATING DIVORCE

After many weeks of therapy, John sat in his counselor's office feeling angry and hurt. He still could not accept that after twelve years of marriage his wife had filed for divorce.

"She didn't give me a chance," he said after several moments of silence. "When she told me six months ago that we were through, I tried so hard to change. I really believed we could work things out. But now as I look back, it's as though she had reached some sort of emotional threshold six months ago. It reminds me of the lyrics from one of the songs in *The Phantom of the Opera*:

> Past the point of no return,
> the final threshold,
> the bridge is crossed,
> so stand and watch it burn . . .
> We've passed the point of no return . . ."*

---

*"The Point Of No Return" from *The Phantom Of The Opera*, Music; Andrew Lloyd Webber; lyrics, Charles Hart; additional lyrics, Richard Stilgoe. Copyright 1986, The Really Useful Group Ltd. Reproduced by kind permission.

After a long pause, John added: "You know, I don't think our relationship failed; I think my wife just stopped trying."

THE POINT OF NO RETURN: THE CUMULATIVE EFFECTS OF MARITAL CONFLICT

John's despair has been echoed by countless men as they ponder the reasons that might have led to a partner's unilateral decision to divorce. Was John correct in assuming that his wife had reached "the point of no return"? If so, what factors pushed her to that "emotional threshold"?

As we saw in the case of Joan in the preceding chapter, the dynamics leading to a woman's marital dissatisfaction often are rooted in her inability to identify and communicate her unsatisfied needs to her husband. Unfortunately, because many women do not assert themselves to discuss these needs when they surface, a woman may simply swallow the pain that accompanies her unmet needs. And when ongoing pain is buried, it accumulates and festers. But with the passage of time, the specific causes of the pain become blurred. When the woman finally awakens to the recognition that "enough is enough," she may not be able to identify specifically the factors that eventually influenced her decision to dissolve the relationship.

Not too many years ago, before "no-fault" divorce became a reality in many states, men and women alike had to go to court with specific complaints or reasons for their irreconcilable differences. Relatives and friends were dragged into court to testify on behalf of the individual seeking the divorce. Partners who lacked legitimate reasons to divorce had to manufacture plausible ones.

Later, when asked why they divorced, they might respond with tongue-in-cheek reasons like "He ate crackers in bed," or "She squeezed the toothpaste at the wrong end of the tube." And whether the person was the "dumper" or the "dumpee," these flippant responses made a mockery of the wrenching pain suffered by those whose marriages had ended. Everyone suffers in some way from the finality of divorce, and the grief associated with the loss of a relationship—even one that has gone sour—is predictable and inescapable.

As in times past, a woman today who has suffered the cumulative effects of marital conflict often has trouble conjuring up a definitive, solid, final justification for seeking a divorce. Feeling as though she has one foot on the pier and one in the boat, she tries to work through her dilemma: "I want out of this marriage, but I don't have a valid reason for getting out. If only he drank, or committed adultery, or were physically violent, it would make my decision so much easier."

Also, it is not uncommon for a woman who represses her anger and resentment about unresolved marital problems to request too late that her husband change. After she has reached the point of no return, when she's lost hope that the differences can be reconciled, any behavioral changes by her husband will likely have little or no positive effect on her. It is not unusual to hear such a woman say, "He's trying very hard to change, but even if he changed completely, I don't think it would make much of a difference anymore."

Let's look at the case of Barbara and Janet, a common scenario that illustrates some of the key issues that surface when women reflect on the snowballing effects of conflict in their marriage.

THE CASE OF BARBARA AND JANET

The attractive, divorced woman in her mid-fifties was sitting across from her young, married friend, Barbara. They had been meeting for lunch on a regular basis since Barbara's marriage began to fall apart several months ago.

The younger woman said, "Janet, it's getting so difficult to stay in my marriage. I've already told you how dreadful our sex life is. There is no romance, there is no loving, there is only sex that has no meaning. He's so absorbed in his work that I feel like I'm a single parent. I'm tired of feeling lonely.

"We can't even carry on a decent conversation anymore. And when we do talk, the discussion usually ends up in an argument. So many things have happened in the past that I've been unable to talk to him about; I'm beginning to think I hate him. I really don't think I want to be married any longer, and most of my friends think I should leave him."

Barbara paused. And then, as though searching for a last straw by which to judge her failing marriage, she asked, "Janet, when did you know your marriage was over?"

"There it is," thought Janet. "The big question: When is enough, enough?" She knew from her own experience the ambivalence her friend was struggling with and the pain Barbara felt as she searched outside herself for reasons to end the marriage.

Flashbacks of her twenty-year marriage flooded Janet's mind. She remembered with a tinge of pleasure her first date with the man who would one day become her husband. She recalled their wedding day, the day each of their four children was born, and their first home. The memories were vivid—year after year of Thanksgiving dinners with her own special recipe for turkey dressing, opening presents on Christmas Eve, and all the rituals and subtle, unwritten expectations and understandings that came to define their family.

It seemed to her that time had dulled the edge of pain and helped her remember with greater compassion the joys of the past. But she wondered if it is really time itself that dulls the pain of the past, or what we do with our time that makes the difference.

But to answer her friend's question, Janet had to search much deeper to recall the painful emotions which, through therapy, she had learned to identify. She remembered the hurt she felt when she learned of her husband's past affairs; the shame she felt when he told her that if she had been a more loving wife, the affairs would not have happened; the hopelessness that resulted when disagreements escalated into arguments that were left unresolved and caused her to bury feelings that erupted later in the form of rage.

She recalled the frustration she felt when expensive family vacations created more distress than relaxation; the emptiness of many lonely years when her husband was working his way up in his profession; the fear she felt when she contemplated life as a divorced woman. And underlying it all was the anxiety that came with the recurrent thoughts that her husband might be right—that it was something she herself was doing to create this monster of a marriage.

How could she explain this complex constellation of reasons? Finally, she said, "It wasn't just one thing, Barbara. It was a series of problems that took me over the edge. It was as though I had collected a coupon for each painful experience over many years. I guess when I collected a sufficient number, I knew intuitively that it was time to cash in those coupons for a divorce."

The conversation of the two women illustrates several dynamics that propel women toward divorce. For example, we see that women tend to interpret the ultimate breakdown of a marriage in terms of not one, but rather a series of disturbances that take them past the point of no return. For women, divorce is often the result of an intuitive decision. And though the decision defies the stringent test of scientific method—there may be no clear-cut cause and effect—once the decision is made, there usually is no turning back.

THE LIMITS OF ROMANCE

Barbara's comment about the "dreadful" state of her sex life and the absence of romance is significant. Romance appears to be far more important to women than to men. However, relationships rooted primarily in romantic love may be filled with self-deception. Romantic love requires that we attach all sorts of qualities of virtue and perfection to the one with whom we are smitten. The loved one may then become almost entirely a creature of our imagination. This illusive veil of fantasy distorts the image of the person with whom we share our love and prevents us from becoming genuinely close to, and intimate with, a partner. The individuals we conceal behind the veil are unable to be authentically themselves and become an extension of our own needs.

Thus, the reason romance is doomed from the very beginning is that the encounter consists of two incomplete people looking to each other to find what is missing within themselves. Loving, on the other hand, is deeply rooted in the love we hold for ourselves—as we really are—as well as the love we hold for the other.

Granted, romantic love has its place. It plays a primary role during courtship. It gives us a rush, and the excitement keeps us coming back for more. The anticipation of being with the object of our romantic love is a "fix" that some of us can easily get hooked on. Recent studies of romantic love indicate that this intoxicating "high" is more than an illusion. When we find ourselves romantically smitten, the brain releases a set of natural amphetamines—dopamine, norepinephrine, and phenylethylamine—which are capable of triggering the "swept away" feelings of euphoria and elation.

Unfortunately, these chemicals are short-lived, and, in time, the body's supply becomes depleted. In the absence of a more mature love between partners, the "rush" of the romantic stage ends. And so does the relationship.

However, romantic love can play a significant role in a marriage based on mature love. Dinner by candlelight, a weekend getaway for two, or roses at the office can add spice to a relationship. But men and women who rely exclusively or extensively on the superficial qualities of romantic love will inevitably come to the realization that the glamorous aura that once surrounded a partner no longer exists. Without a more intimate level of emotionally shared love, romance can be hollow, expendable, and easily sacrificed in the wake of life's stresses and strains. The demise of romance is painfully apparent when we search the card racks for an anniversary card that accurately reflects the way we feel toward our spouse!

What is the alternative to illusive romance? To build a genuine, nonillusive, loving and emotionally supportive relationship, seven basic emotional needs must be met. They are the needs for love, caring, understanding, respect, appreciation, acceptance, and trust.[1] Unlike individuals who are hooked on romantic love, the healthy couple communicates these basic needs in a way that does not enslave them or blind them from reality. When two people do not learn to effectively communicate their emotional love needs, they have set up destructive deterrents to healthy, loving, and growing relationships.

If a loving relationship is our goal, both partners must first make a mutual commitment to the seven basic attitudes of loving, as well as develop the physical and verbal communication skills that fulfill those needs for each other. The expression of our sexuality and affection through sex then becomes the frosting on the cake of shared loving needs. Otherwise, sex may become simply a mechanical act that accomplishes little more than the satisfaction of a basic biological drive. Sexual intimacy, under these circumstances, will not communicate a shared expression of healthy, mature love.

THE PAIN OF LONELINESS

The story of Barbara and Janet further illustrates the loneliness many married women feel as their needs go unmet. Paradoxically, loneliness also appears to be one of the things feared by both men and women who are contemplating separation or divorce. A group of such men and women were asked by a therapist, "What things do you fear most when you envision yourself as a divorced person?" The majority gave two of the same responses: "Being alone, and financial difficulties." However, the men and women ranked the two responses in reverse order, with being alone ranking first for the women.

As we discussed this issue further, the clients said that it was not really being alone that they feared most, but, rather feeling lonely. In fact, most of them admitted that being alone—and finally enjoying some peace and quiet away from the stresses of the marriage—would have been a welcome gift! In talking about this fear of loneliness, these men and women were struck by the discovery that they had experienced much loneliness in the marriage they were thinking of leaving. They were very fearful of suffering the depressive symptoms of loneliness once they were separated and/or divorced. In short, they knew well the pain of loneliness and were adamant about not wanting to experience it again after divorce.

One wonders if a desire to escape from loneliness is the catalyst that drives divorced men and women into remarriage prematurely. Recent statistics on remarriage in the United States today reflect not only the popularity of remarriage but also its vulnerability: 70 percent of divorced men and women—one million each year—remarry. Yet 60 percent of these remarriages end in divorce.[2]

THE TALKING CURE

The case of Barbara and Janet also points to an important distinction between men and women: Women talk to each other about even their most intimate problems. Most men do not. When women experience difficulties, under most conditions they confide in each other. Men have no similar venting outlet, and even their closest friends may be completely unaware that a problem exists.

Furthermore, when a wife tries to tell her husband about a problem she is experiencing, she most likely is looking for caring, nurturing, and supportive encouragement. In short, she wants to experience intimacy. However, because men tend to be problem solvers, her husband's agenda may well include a litany of ways she can eliminate the problem.

One woman who had been married for several years remarked that she had tried to alleviate some of her resentment toward her husband by inviting him out to an elegant restaurant for dinner. Her agenda, she said, included discussing ways they might develop a closer relationship. She had in mind a spontaneous, give-and-take discussion, in which each of them could express their needs in a quiet, comfortable atmosphere. To her dismay, as soon as they were seated at their table, her husband reached into his jacket pocket and pulled out a large sheet of paper on which he had listed, in concrete terms, exactly what she needed to do to help improve their relationship!

Though this man cannot be admonished for not taking his wife's request seriously (and, with due respect to him, he had, indeed, done his homework), he missed a very important point that many men in our society overlook: He lacked the awareness that when a woman has a problem she wishes to "discuss," more often than not she wants to be touched, held, and listened to with empathy and concern. Oftentimes, the product-oriented man does not understand that the process-oriented woman really is talking about problems *in order to get close* and not to get to solutions.

And so, when a woman asserts herself to invite her husband to "talk," and he produces a list of twenty ways to solve a problem, the process is destroyed. She will likely shift the gears in her brain from forward to reverse, mutter under her breath, "He just doesn't understand what I am trying to tell him," and, as soon as possible, telephones her girlfriend, who surely will listen and know what she is going through.

Women are, indeed, intuitive, and, because our motives for engaging in conversation and our style of communicating are similar, we seem to have a collective sense of what other women are looking for. As we saw in Barbara's case, when women contemplate divorce, they seek validation and support from other women. This "talking cure" serves the important function of increasing the sense of intimacy a woman feels through connection with someone who is like her.

As Deborah Tannen points out in her book, *You Just Don't Understand: Women and Men in Conversation*,[3] for women who talk about a problem, the message may not be the main point of complaining. Instead, it is what Tannen calls the underlying "metamessage" that cuts to the core of the latent, hidden meaning behind her words. Hence, when a woman talks about her problems and then feels empathy from another woman who conveys the metamessage, "I know how you feel; you're not alone," a warmth and closeness result from the sense that she is understood.

When a man gives advice to a woman in order to "help" her solve her problems, he misses an important opportunity to receive and provide complementary rapport and caring. Instead, the man who offers solutions sends a powerful signal that suggests he is more knowledgeable, more reasonable, and more in control than the woman.

In addition, a man must learn to understand that when he engages in conversation with a woman, she is very sensitive to metamessages that transcend mere words. And, though he may be completely oblivious to the tone of his voice or his body language, these elements can also influence the way in which she interprets what he says. Hence, metamessages that do not convey support, encouragement, and understanding can close down communication, push the woman away, and become the breeding ground for feelings of aloneness and loneliness. By not recognizing the potentially destructive metamessages he may be sending, a man can subjugate a woman through condescension and one-upmanship and chip away at the very core of her sense of self-worth.

Talking about our frustrations to others serves an additional purpose for women: It helps us process out loud the abundance of pertinent information that will, in the end, guide us toward a decision. Unlike men, who seem to be able to accomplish the decision-making process quite effectively in the silence of their minds, women appear to need the medium of verbal communication in order to achieve the task.

We see, then, that a number of factors can escalate marital dissatisfaction and crest with the decision to divorce. However, working with these dynamics is another significant and powerful phenomenon: the cumulative process of predictable and definable divorce stages.

While the decision to divorce is rarely a mutual and simultaneous one for wife and husband, the spouses generally do share a common agreement about the condition of their marriage. However, they may not recognize the extent of the deterioration that exists within their relationship. If couples understand the divorce process as a sequence of stages and can identify where their marriage fits on the continuum, they will be better able to assess how much energy they must expend to alter the direction their marriage has taken. Such an awareness may help save the marriage.

Individuals contemplating divorce will likely reach a "point of no return" the farther they progress along the continuum. Stated another way, as the couple moves through the stages, the potential for reversing the process diminishes, and the incentive to change weakens. Perhaps John's observation at the beginning of this chapter was correct: Marriages don't fail; at some point people just stop trying.

THE STAGES OF CUMULATIVE DIVORCE

Wayne E. Oates has identified six stages of cumulative divorce.[4] In order to bring these stages into sharper focus, we will describe the struggles that are associated with each emerging stage. Keep in mind that at any stage in the cumulative divorce continuum, consultation with an experienced therapist can help reverse the process.

Stage One: Conflict in Adjustment

According to Oates, marital discord that arises during the earliest years of marriage centers on the establishment of the partners' mutual understanding of their roles, routines, idiosyncratic habits and rituals, along with an elaborate system of verbal and nonverbal clues. It is during this critical period that they begin to realize that very important differences, previously hidden, exist between them.

Differences may emerge, for example, in the following areas: the couple's understanding of intimacy; the role of work, relaxation, and recreation in their lives; how they resolve conflict, deal with stress, and communicate; philosophies about child rearing practices; same- and opposite-sex friendships outside the marriage; and their need for independence and freedom. If the love relationship is to grow, the partners must examine each of these areas in an atmosphere of mutual respect and empathic understanding.

During this early period of adjustment, couples can learn a great deal about each other from participating in marriage retreats and/or talking with other married people who have learned to acknowledge and accept their differences. In addition, reading books that explain male and female psychological differences can prevent the resentment and rejection that arise when these differences are misunderstood.

For example, John Gray's book, *Men, Women and Relationships: Making Peace With the Opposite Sex,*[5] is an excellent guide to enriching relationships. It encourages partners to accept the reality that, indeed, differences do exist between the sexes in a number of critical areas, and that these differences need not place men and women in adversarial positions. Partners can read one chapter at a time, and, before moving on to the next, can discuss the issues raised that may be creating problems in their relationship.

When partners read this book and understand the major differences that exist between the sexes, four important changes generally occur: (1) Each partner becomes more accepting of the other's differences; (2) each individual stops expecting the opposite sex to be more like himself or herself; (3) each individual becomes more relaxed, and the resentment toward the other partner, as well as the need to change that person, begins to dissipate; and (4) the relationship reaches a new level of intimacy because the partners are able to be who they genuinely are, as opposed to who they are expected to be.

Although a number of issues surface during the early adjustment stage of marriage, three areas frequently produce conflict: boundary issues with families of origin, intimacy issues, and issues related to dependence, independence, and interdependence. Unless these areas of conflict are examined and understood early in the relationship, defensiveness and resentment can start the downward spiral of marital dissatisfaction.

Boundary Issues. The early state of marital adjustment is a time for partners to take a critical look at the boundaries they have established with their biological families. This is necessary so they may begin to establish for their partnership a healthy sense of separateness from their families of origin. This need is particularly acute for young people who move directly from living with their biological families to living with their marriage partners. However, establishing a healthy detachment also applies to those who have chosen to remain single for a long period of time. Whether these "marrying-later" adults live on their own, have returned home many times, or have never left home, the need for emotional and/or financial support often keeps these men and women dependent on their biological families. It appears reasonable to assume that the longer the dependency, the more enmeshed the family network becomes. Freeing themselves from unhealthy over-connectedness can become a monumental letting-go task for these individuals.

Unhealthy fusion with the biological family is also a danger for the woman who goes through divorce and eventually remarries. When a woman separates and divorces, she usually progresses through a grief period in which she tries to come to terms with her sense of loss. This period, which will be described in detail later, can last for many months. It is during this time that the self-absorbed pain of divorce, which may bring on feelings of insecurity and mistrust, yearns to be soothed. Her need for comfort, security, and trust may drive her to reattach to her biological family. Some divorced women return, either physically and/or emotionally, to their families of origin, even when it is apparent that the women are products of dysfunctional families, which continue to function in unhealthy ways.

If a woman remarries following a period of reattachment to her family of origin, one of her major tasks will be to actively redefine boundaries between the generations. If she does not, and she remains fused to her biological family, she severely hampers her ability to develop a sense of autonomy as a person and to establish her new marital relationship as a distinct and separate entity.

Intimacy. The pursuit of a healthy, intimate relationship is an important psychosocial task of adulthood. Without intimacy, an individual can be destined for a life of isolation, hopelessness, and despair. However, many factors create barriers for people as they attempt to build lasting, intimate relationships. Among those barriers are the vulnerability, mistrust, anger, and depression suffered through the loss of previous relationships; the wounds incurred from early, unhealthy family-of-origin patterns; relationships that lack commitment; codependency issues; and sex, alcohol, drug, and other addictions.

Exploration of these barriers to intimacy have had an explosive impact with the publishing industry responding to the demand. Today, there are so many self-help books in bookstores that they are frequently classified according to illness rather than author. For many of us, these books have replaced the guidance once found in newspaper horoscopes, Chinese fortune cookies, and day calendars. And while there are some excellent books on the shelves, they should be read with a critical eye and not to the exclusion of other equally productive activities.

One divorced woman lamented, "I have read every book available about how I can develop a more intimate relationship. But now I realize that I was spending so much time reading, I wasn't taking the time to develop an intimate relationship!" Self-help books are effective only to the extent that we translate the knowledge into action and behavioral change. Reading is like playing solitaire—we do it alone. And without subsequent action and change from within, reading may become an exercise in futility.

During the early marital adjustment period, many women complain that they are unable to derive from their husbands the quality of intimacy they had been promised and now long for. Many admit that the harder they have tried to achieve intimacy with their marriage partners, the more distant their husbands have become. Some then try, unsuccessfully, to discover intimacy in extramarital relationships. They become those porous rocks described earlier, absorbing nourishment from the external world to fill their emptiness. What is not understood, by men and

women alike, is that intimacy is the result of a sense of wholeness—the seeds of which lie not in the other, but within ourselves. And as long as we look beyond ourselves to find intimacy, we can neither have it nor share it. Intimacy is discovered
within ourselves by knowing who we are: what we think, what
we feel, what we want, and what we value. When we know these
things about ourselves, we are ready to be intimate with another
individual.

Intimacy, then, is not a commodity that we can simply ask
for; it is not something that just happens. Intimacy is not "created
in heaven." And, it is not something that we can ever achieve
without a keen awareness of our real selves and a positive attitude toward that self. Intimacy is directly related to the degree to
which a woman has developed confidence in her identity and a
sense of individuality as a separate, whole person.

As Harriet Goldhor Lerner points out in her book *The
Dance of Intimacy*, the challenge of intimacy requires being an
assertive, separate, independent, authentic self. It requires having
the courage to be ourselves while, at the same time, staying
"emotionally connected to that other party who thinks, feels and
believes differently, without needing to change, convince, or fix
the other."[6]

In short, if we have the courage to first come to know our
deepest nature and to reveal that nature to another human being,
the separateness of each individual is then capable of forming a
spiritually centered connectedness. It is in this way that the existential core of two human beings—their spirits and their souls—
finds new meaning.

Dependence/Independence/Interdependence. As the foregoing discussion has suggested, it is only when we move away
from our dependency on others to satisfy our need for intimacy,
that we are free to develop a healthy state of independence. This
new state creates in us a sense of self-directedness, self-reliance,

and responsibility for our own lives. When we are able to achieve this mature sense of independence, we stop chastising others for their inadequacies. We stop criticizing them for their mistakes, we stop blaming them for what they don't give us, and we no longer depend on others to give us what we fear we are unable to provide for ourselves.

Thus, when we have achieved a mature sense of independence, we are then free to choose to be with someone because the quality of our life as a healthy, whole person is enhanced, and we choose that other person out of love, not out of fear.

Once we move from dependence to independence, we are then able to continue on our journey toward a healthy state of interdependence. In his book *The Seven Habits of Highly Effective People: Powerful Lessons in Personal Change,*[7] Stephen Covey discusses the "Maturity Continuum" from dependence to independence to interdependence. Covey points out that as infants we are totally dependent on others. Without food, shelter, and nurturing, directed and sustained by others, we would live only a few hours. During this stage on the maturity continuum, the small child depends on the paradigm of "you;" that is, I expect you to take care of me, and I will blame you if you don't.

If the child is able to grow and develop in a healthy way, the dependent "you" changes to an independent "I;" I can do it, I can choose. Interdependence is the paradigm of "we;" we can do it, we can cooperate, and we can do something together. Consequently, dependent people can get what they want only from others. Independent people don't rely on others to get what they want. Interdependent people, on the other hand, use their resources in combination with those of others in order to achieve what neither might have achieved alone.

Interdependence between partners has at its very heart a sense of unconditional positive regard for a partner—even when we are acutely aware that, as people, we are very different in many ways. This unconditional, nonpossessive, nonjudgmental, and tolerant attitude toward a partner gives that person the fullest opportunity to express feelings and thoughts openly without pretense or defense. Hence, as interdependence develops and grows during the initial stage of marital adjustment, it brings with it the hope that partners will develop the freedom to be different and to communicate that difference authentically and confidently. As adapted from the book *Loving Free*, freedom then becomes:

> . . . the reward for two people who can be completely open. It's the freedom for a man to cry on a woman's shoulder when he needs to cry, yet be a man. It's the freedom to tell you the worst things I see in myself and know that you won't abandon me or destroy me with criticism. It's knowing that no demands will ever be made on our privacy, that there will be no prying or forcing of disclosures that aren't ready to be revealed. It's knowing that the truth can always be told, and that no matter how painful it is, someone is trying to understand and accept it. It's knowing that loneliness will never be a part of our lives again. There is someone who really cares how we feel.
>
> It's never fearing that we will be misunderstood. Given enough time, we can help each other really hear what we are saying. It's the freedom to be free, to be part of someone else and still be ourselves, to be totally secure, knowing that we are anchored in trust. It's never being taken for granted again. It's never again feeling that one role in life is superior or more important than another. It's a partnership with two people deeply committed to each other, trying to do their jobs to the best of their ability, and knowing that each is appreciated fully by the other.
>
> Most important, it's the confidence, the peace of knowing that we never stand alone when confronted with any problem. It's recognizing that the world can't touch us, can't hurt us, can't pull us down, as long as we have each other. And that no single force, except death, is greater than our strength combined.[8]

Such a mature sense of freedom, which springs from a

couple's development toward interdependence, is likely to exist only in embryonic form during the early years of marriage. However, when it is absent entirely, and/or when partners do not recognize that movement toward interdependence is a critical developmental task, the couple might progress to the next stage of the divorce continuum.

Stage Two: The Collapse of the Covenant of Trust and Withdrawal of Selves

During this stage, the couple's covenant of trust and intimacy is broken as one of the partners discovers something damaging about the other. The effect of discovery is usually withdrawal from the offending spouse, and, ultimately, both partners from each other. At this stage, any thoughts about divorcing the offending partner are usually nonverbal; yet, each partner is cognizant of the unspoken threat of marital rupture.

The new truth that is discovered can come in a variety of forms. For example, the covenant of trust can collapse when a partner discovers his or her spouse:

- is gay

- has entered the marriage with extraordinary debts

- was previously married

- is having an extramarital affair

- has a prison record

- has not worked through a previous divorce and/or has not "let go" of a previous marital partner

- has a child from a previous marriage

Revelation of any one of these situations—and others like

them—can be extremely traumatic for both men and women. Yet, if such a discovery can be defined with some degree of clarity and specificity, it is possible for the couple to work through the problems that the discovery has caused.

However, some revelations are not so concrete and precise; we might call them "existential predicaments." Their effect on a marriage can be quite chilling and can restrict the potential for positive change. One of the most serious of these occurs when a partner announces that the marriage has lost its vitality and excitement and that he or she has "fallen out of love." Though this threat to the covenant of trust is less likely to happen during the early years of marriage, it is a contemporary dilemma that can occur at just about any stage. This announcement poses a serious threat to the marriage, as it can trigger a sense of hopelessness in both partners. Furthermore, it often precipitates feelings of self-blame in the offended partner, while the spouse may experience enormous feelings of guilt.

Let's examine, as a typical example, the collapse of the covenant of trust that follows the discovery of a husband's infidelity.

When a woman discovers that her husband has had, or is having, an extramarital affair, the sense of loss she experiences can trigger an unprecedented emotional response. Her condition can be worsened when, as in Janet's case at the beginning of this chapter, her husband tells her that if she had been a more loving wife, the adulterous behavior would not have occurred. In this case, the offending partner fails to understand that blaming the victim for what one freely chooses to do is, at best, an irresponsible by-product of self-deception.

If the wife internalizes feelings of blame and guilt about her husband's infidelity, she then adds self-punishment to: 1) the stress she already feels regarding the potential for contracting a sexually transmitted disease; 2) the threat she has suffered to her ego; 3) the anxiety and fear she feels about no longer being lovable or able to love; and 4) the despair she experiences as a rejected woman.

How does a wife cope with such a discovery? The woman may react to her husband's behavior by blaming herself and turning her anger inward. Or, she may express her anger directly to the one who has inflicted the pain. But the unavoidable question that haunts her is: "Will I ever be able to trust my husband again?" In time she may be able to assume a position of "guarded trust" and thereby stop the progression toward divorce. This response seems to depend to a large extent upon the degree to which she has been deceived, when the affair occurred, and the proximity of the "other woman."

For example, the intensity of a wife's emotional response may depend on whether the other woman is someone with whom her husband had a brief liaison years ago at an out-of-town conference, or whether he is currently having an affair with his secretary or the teller who calls you by your first name at the bank.

In addition to the factors of deception, timing, and proximity, how a woman deals with her feelings about the breach of trust can have a direct effect on the future of the marriage. For example, the eventual decision to divorce appears far more likely for the woman who openly expresses her anger than it is for the woman who internalizes feelings of guilt and self-blame for her husband's wrongdoing. From the husband's point of view, generating feelings of guilt in the offended spouse can be a very effective, though emotionally destructive, tool for a man who has no desire to leave his marriage.

Likewise, women may consciously suppress their anger and use their husband's offense to benefit themselves, or use it as a weapon to control their husband. In addition, fears about future loneliness, anxieties about finances or the ability to be an effective single parent, concerns about competing in the job market or completing their education, and even the threat of having to leave the comforts of a nice home, may work separately or together to prevent some women from considering divorce.

When women decide, for whatever reason, to remain in a relationship in which the covenant of trust has been breached, using their husband's offense as a manipulative ploy to get their external needs met, this decision can create additional suffering. When women compromise their integrity by "selling out," they often manifest symptoms of clinical depression as they experience the negative effects of anger, guilt, and diminished self-worth. Women who take responsibility and become accountable for the choices they are making—even choices that keep them in a relationship that is no longer ideal—face a major challenge as they take a significant first step in recovering from a breach of trust.

When the covenant of trust collapses and the conflict is not resolved, partners often become so unresponsive to one another that physical and emotional withdrawal can follow. Unfortunately, as partners proceed to live as though an invisible line partitions the home into separate "his and her" zones, the children in the family notice and are affected. They begin to form mental images of what relationships between men and women are supposed to be like. These images are filed away in the children's minds, to be retrieved much later when they develop their own relationships. Once set in motion, this cycle of dysfunction can be perpetuated across generations. That is, dysfunctional people tend to gravitate toward other dysfunctional people, and, once married, they pass on to their offspring the patterns that will be repeated in future relationships.

Children can also become the recipients of other forms of emotional injury. In a family where the father and mother have become polarized, children may become the targets of displaced aggression. Perhaps anger toward the spouse is repressed, because one parent fears retribution, loss of love and/or security, abandonment, total loss of control, or loss of other benefits that are external to the relationship but are valued. When parents are unable to focus on the real cause of their anger, they may vent that anger on their powerless and vulnerable children.

Conversely, when partners withdraw their loyalties to the marital relationship and no longer give and receive spousal love, it may be very difficult for them to resist the impulse to cross over the healthy physical and emotional boundaries they previously had with their children. Youngsters, then, become the targets of their parents' misdirected love needs and may become spoiled and pampered. Even worse, they may become trapped in an emotionally incestuous relationship with one or both parents.

If couples do not seek professional help to resolve the issues that surface during this stage, further movement toward divorce is expected and predictable, as family problems escalate.

Stage Three: The Stage of Private Foreboding

The problems that emerged during the second stage of the cumulative divorce continuum are intensified during stage three. During this stage, there is a sense of threat as each partner becomes acutely aware that at any moment the other spouse may voice what until now has been unspoken.

The woman who resolves not to talk about her marital problems to those close to her suffers in silence. If she lacks a healthy outlet for venting her feelings, her symptoms of depression can escalate. In addition, symptoms such as indecisiveness and an inability to focus her attention can worsen her conflict, preventing her from concentrating on what to do about her marriage and how to go about doing it. As a result, women often become "stuck," and their feelings of hopelessness and helplessness at this stage may intensify.

This can be a very difficult time for women. As they begin to experience a "living-together-apart" existence with their spouses, they may also begin to engage in more activities without their partners. These women must then confront the stark reality that there is a premium placed on being coupled in our society. Particularly for the woman whose identity has been defined by her marital relationship, the thought of being single in a couples' world can be a serious threat to her feelings of security and self-worth. And, as her anxiety level increases, along with her recognition of being alone, she may become acutely aware of such things as:

- the man who holds the door open for a woman

- the woman who is helped with her coat

- the man who pumps gasoline while a woman sits waiting inside the car

- the man who wears no ring on the third finger of his left hand

- the number of women who sit alone in church on Sunday mornings

- the number of men and women, who didn't know her husband well, who now "miss" him when he is not in her company

- the countless number of men and women who walk hand in hand in public.

Even scenes in the movies may take on new meaning, reflecting the love/hate ambivalence she may be feeling about her husband. A love scene may strike her as revolting, or, on the other hand, it may make her long for what is missing in her life.

The woman who is progressing through this private stage of the divorce continuum also may seek a silent form of validation from other women who are divorced. The message she seeks is: "Nice women sometimes do get divorced and they do survive the breakup."

This stage is also capable of producing a deep contradiction within the woman whose internal struggle is not consistent with what she wants the external world to see in her. On one hand she feels, "I'm miserable; I have an enormous conflict going on in my life; I need support." However, the image she shows the world is, "I'm fine; I don't have a problem; I don't need anyone's advice." This discrepancy acts as a mask, preventing her from feeling genuine and real. As the conflict between her inner reality and her distorted projections to the outside world creates discomfort, her more sensitive friends, relatives, and co-workers may sense that something is wrong. Generally, however, any attempt to support the woman is met with resistance until she has stepped across the point of no return and is ready to confide in someone.

As we saw in the case of Barbara at the beginning of the chapter, a woman's motivation to talk about her marital conflict to another person is enhanced if the listener is perceived to be an empathic person who communicates genuine understanding. When this relationship of confidence is established, and the woman is able to shed her defensive mask and speak openly about her "secret," she has entered the fourth stage of the cumulative divorce sequence.

Stage Four: Going Public—The Stage of Social Involvement

This stage is a critical turning point in the process of marital dissolution. At this juncture, members of a person's extended family, as well as close friends, become aware of the "secret."

The people in whom a woman confides, and their responses to her conflict, can have a profound effect on both her emotional well-being and the direction she decides to take. For example, if there are children and the woman's parents and/or in-laws are consulted, these grandparents may urge her to keep the family together for the sake of the children. If she does, the grandparents are not forced to take on new roles within the family system, which might include becoming caretakers for their grandchildren.

Though divorce as a cure for marital discord may be much harder on the children than is the conflict itself, couples who stay together only for the sake of the children may be deluding themselves. This is similar to the self-deception of unhappy partners who choose to have a child in hopes of improving the quality of their lives together. These people are missing an important point: Children can become as severely damaged when living in an unhealthy, unhappy home environment as they can when they are products of divorce.

The age of a child, the particular developmental stage the child is in, and the nature and intensity of the marital discord must be taken into consideration. However, a child's ability to cope effectively with the grief of separation and divorce is improved when:

- a child has developed a sense of personal self-worth long before the divorce

- the parents of the child are able to cope effectively with the breakup of their marriage

- the parents are able to work cooperatively together on divorce-related issues

(Chapter Six examines the effects of divorce on children and the measures that can be taken to help them through the process.)

When a woman tells members of her extended family that she is experiencing pain in her marriage, she may get another response. People who care about her will want to spare her grief; therefore, it is not unusual for relatives to advise the woman to leave the situation that is creating the anguish. For example, when a woman who feels betrayed by her spouse confides in loved ones, she may be told: "Well, then leave him before you're hurt any more," or "Leave him before he finds another woman," or "Leave him while you're still young enough to start a new life."

These well-meaning people inevitably become part of the problem rather than part of the solution. A woman may already feel vulnerable, and she may be so susceptible to the suggestions of others that she acts upon the advice she hears without regard for other options.

In addition, when a woman talks to relatives who are emotionally enmeshed with her, she may place herself in a no-win situation. On the one hand, if she heeds their advice and leaves her husband, she passes up opportunities to examine options that might keep the marriage together. On the other hand, if she chooses to stay and the marriage doesn't work out, she may then have to live with the family's comments or unspoken insinuations of "I told you so." This can intensify any self-blame or feelings of shame, guilt, or mental anguish she may already be experiencing.

Other problems can arise at this stage if, rather than confiding in a caring female friend or, even better, a pastor or a therapist, a woman chooses to tell her "secret" to a male friend. When a person of the opposite sex listens empathically to another person whose marriage is collapsing and who is feeling the absence of love and caring, it is often only a matter of time before a sexual relationship develops. These relationships can become lethal, because the woman may begin to feel guilty for having reversed her role from that of "victim" to "perpetrator." And, what's more, the sexual liaison can occur at a time when she has not devoted sufficient energy to resolving the problems that threaten her marriage. Hence, when women are tempted to enter a sexual relationship before the dissolution of their marriage and before the successful resolution of their psychological conflicts, the new relationship is likely to self-destruct before long.

Some people tend to be drawn with magnetic force to those whose psychological and emotional problems reflect their own.

Thus, those with impaired ability to function in relationships tend to gravitate toward other dysfunctional people. This phenomenon adds another level of meaning to the profound words of cartoonist Walt Kelly's Pogo: "We have met the enemy, and he is us."

Stage Five: Threats of Separation and Divorce

By the time a couple reaches the fifth stage of the divorce continuum, the bitterness may be so great and the communication so poor that the only thing each can see clearly in the other's character is the partner's darker side. Reversing the progression of marital dissolution at this point can be a monumental task. However, when "divorce talk" is introduced, the offended partner may urge the spouse to participate in marriage counseling.

It is apparent why the victimized partner would wish to participate in counseling. However, there are also a number of reasons why the partner who wants out might be agreeable to seek professional help. For example, though some partners say they want to leave their spouse, what they really want to do is vent their anger and punish the other person. They might view the therapy setting as an opportunity to do so.

Others participate in counseling because they do, indeed, want out of the relationship, but they want to solicit the support of a therapist in order to make it easier to leave the marriage. Others are adamant about wanting a divorce and want no part of marriage counseling, but they participate to show good faith to, among other people, their children, their extended family, or an extramarital partner. And still others go because they want to be absolutely sure they have exhausted every option for mending the relationship before they decide to leave it.

During this stage, a number of factors can affect a couple's chances for reversing the destructive downward spiral of marital breakup. Among these are the severity of distress, age of the partners, emotional disengagement, and incompatibility. Let's take a closer look at each of these factors.

The severity of distress. The level of commitment to a relationship by each partner is a significant factor in determining the severity of distress a couple may be experiencing. The question that brings the issue into focus is this: Has the conflict progressed so far that the partners have reached the point of no return and are no longer willing to make a commitment to the marriage? In other words, is the marriage deadlocked, dying, or dead? The severity of distress in the marriage is likely to be greater if either of the partners has sought legal advice or has retained a lawyer with the intention of taking the initial steps toward seeking a divorce. Conversely, if both partners are committed to staying in the marriage and working out their problems, their power to negotiate differences becomes greater, and the potential for saving their marriage increases.

Age of the partners. While there are exceptions to the adage that "you can't teach old dogs new tricks," there is some evidence that the older the couple, the less likely they are to be willing to work on improving their marriage. Older couples may have endured years and years of unhappiness, and any threats of divorce at this stage generally become muted. The individuals may have retreated to the stage of private foreboding, living in bitter silence "together-apart," filled with memories of the past, and choked by limited hope for the future. Their fear of starting over is very real, and they may stay together out of commitment, obligation, loyalty, and/or convenience.

What appears to help younger people is their hope for the future. When individuals marry, they not only marry their partners, they marry the wishes they want to fulfill as married people. This is why partners suffer such a sense of loss in a divorce. Whether the person is the offender or the offended, when a relationship dies, so do the hopes and dreams for the future that were invested in the relationship. Any preconceived notions about the future that were tied with the knot of matrimony die with the divorce decree.

To younger people, life lies ahead. But to older people, for whom most of life lies behind, the potential for reversing marital conflict is very difficult. It is impossible to look ahead when you are constantly looking backward.

Emotional disengagement. We can think of emotional disengagement as the absence of that essential "glue" that holds a marriage together. One way to measure emotional disengagement is the frequency—or lack thereof—of sexual contact between the partners. Also, whether the partners argue or avoid conflict entirely can indicate their level of emotional detachment. Animosity is actually healthier in a relationship than apathy, because people are at least connecting when anger replaces silent indifference.

Incompatibility. If partners share the same or similar views about what it takes to make a healthy marriage work, they are more likely to coexist harmoniously. If not, incompatibility results. Problems also arise when the partners' values have, over time, changed in significant ways. For example, one contemporary factor that can create marital incompatibility is the housewife's decision to break away from traditional stereotypic behavior. Enrolling in college or becoming gainfully employed in the marketplace can change gender-role expectations and upset the balance of the family. The value and importance placed upon being a homemaker, which were previously shared by her husband, her family, and herself, become compromised when new options are available to her. The change can plunge the marriage into a quagmire of turmoil.

Finally, the voice that threatens separation or divorce is one that generally is taken very seriously. The message may come from the spouse who has already crossed the point of no return, and the threat will get the attention of the other partner. He or she may struggle to understand and will raise questions about the nature of the conflict. As in the case of John at the beginning of the chapter, valiant attempts at behavioral change may be made in order to preserve the marriage. But changing behavior under these conditions only fosters feelings of compliance, which can create enormous resentment for the offended person. A partner cannot expect to shape and mold another person into compliance, nor can a person shape or mold oneself to pacify another person without damaging effects to the ego. Similarly, we cannot force another into loving if there is no love, nor compel or manipulate another into remaining in a marriage that has died.

However, what people can do when their marriage is threatened is seek counseling in order to exhaust all possible options before making a final decision to dissolve the marriage. Divorce can lead to later regret, particularly if it is done without a great deal of introspection and regard for all the people involved.

When we divorce, we divorce our dreams for the future. We also divorce our children from the world they once knew. We divorce our in-laws and we divorce our mutual friends, who, as most women later come to discover, generally gravitate toward ex-husbands after the divorce. With all the losses that are suffered, partners who later are able to free themselves of guilt and shame are usually those who have struggled and searched for all the plausible ways they might have prevented a breakup. After divorce, these people seldom look backward, asking the "What if" questions: "What if I had tried this . . ." or "What if I had been more . . ." Instead, these people can look themselves in the mirror each morning and say confidently, "I did everything I could to behave responsibly, to struggle with the big questions, and to face the answers honestly and with integrity, and I feel I left no stone unturned."

Stage Six: The Legal Phase

The final stage of the divorce continuum rushes in on a tidal wave of questions about finances and child custody. Emotions run high during this phase of the divorce sequence, and the quality of communication likely will change, affecting everyone in the household. The children begin to feel pulled into the middle of a battle zone that has implications for their future well-being. Even those partners who have amicably and mutually decided to end the marriage may find themselves squabbling with each other over minutiae, such as who gets the antique spittoon that Aunt Gert sent last year for Christmas.

At this point, a trial separation for several weeks or months might be a good way to help the partners independently sort out their feelings. A time-out period can also help them re-evaluate the wisdom behind taking immediate steps to dissolve the relationship. However, if the person who wants out of the marriage takes up residence at another address, the separation may encourage social involvement and complicated entanglements with people of the opposite sex.

The overall advantage of attempting a trial separation can best be determined by considering the reasons for the marital discord, the integrity of the partners, and the age of the children in the household. Particularly if children are involved, the success of a trial separation depends on the degree to which each partner can trust that the other will behave responsibly. Children are deeply affected by the exodus of a parent from the home. If this parent becomes involved with another person, problems are compounded for children and for the parent who is left behind, which can intensify his or her feelings of abandonment and anger. Eventually, whether during a trial separation prior to actual divorce proceedings, or following the divorce itself, children inevitably must deal with the departure of a parent from the family home.

In this chapter we have considered those issues that surface with regularity when a couple contemplates divorce. We have explored the cumulative process of divorce with both a case study and an approach that looks at marital dissolution as a progression of stages.

Since divorce is seldom an impulsive, split second decision, this chapter is intended to help women more clearly understand how the accumulation of conflict can occur, and what issues need to be dealt with before women cross the point of no return.

We have also examined the cumulative divorce continuum from the perspective of the sequence of six stages. By understanding these stages of the divorce sequence, women can get a clearer picture of where they find themselves on the continuum. They are then better able to understand what they are experiencing, what lies ahead, and what it will take to reverse the movement toward divorce.

The chapter that follows provides an overview of the most critical legal and financial questions that arise when divorce is unavoidable. The information is intended to help women become well-informed participants in the legal process. The procedures and the legal jargon often leave women feeling confused, intimidated, and powerless. Yet the decisions that result from this legal process have a profound impact on a woman's future and that of her children. By becoming informed, active participants in the process, women can maximize their potential for receiving fair and equal treatment under the law. And by understanding the financial implications of divorce, they will be better prepared to protect themselves and their children from economic disaster.

CHECKLIST 1

Below are eighteen statements to help you detect the extent to which you are experiencing the major issues that were presented in Chapter Two. The checklist should be completed after reading the chapter and is designed to be used only as a guide to improve your knowledge about yourself, your partner, and your marriage.

This checklist also can serve as a useful tool for recognizing some important differences in perception between you and your partner. By asking your spouse to complete the checklist and then comparing your answers, the differences and similarities in your responses can serve as a beginning point for meaningful discussion.

Again, a word of caution: Without the benefit of a professional, you will probably not understand why you think, feel, or behave the way you do. Therefore, remember to focus on the how's, what's, where's, and when's and not the why's.

Directions: Read each statement carefully and, using the following key, indicate to the left how true it is for you.

1 = Not at all true
2 = Somewhat true
3 = Moderately true
4 = Considerably true
5 = Extremely true

☐ 1. Sometimes I feel angry, but I don't know why.

☐ 2. When my spouse behaves in ways that bother me, I usually explain to him what is troubling me.

☐ 3. My spouse is very romantic.

☐ 4. I wish my spouse and I could share a more intimate level of emotional love.

☐ 5. My spouse is able to effectively communicate a loving attitude toward me.

☐ 6. My spouse is deeply interested in my well-being.

☐ 7. My spouse has an understanding attitude toward me.

☐ 8. My spouse respects me as a person.

☐ 9. My spouse appreciates me.

☐ 10. My spouse accepts me for the person I am.

☐ 11. My spouse trusts me.

☐ 12. I rarely feel lonely.

☐ 13. I wish my spouse would share more private, intimate thoughts with me.

☐ 14. When I want to discuss a problem, my spouse listens with empathy and concern.

☐ 15. When I "trouble talk," my spouse provides solutions and doesn't seem to listen.

☐ 16. When I have a problem, I feel my close friends are more understanding than my spouse.

☐ 17. I have a need to "think out loud" in order to reach a decision.

☐ 18. My spouse has stopped trying to work on our relationship.

CHECKLIST 2

Directions: Use the key found at the beginning of the previous checklist to respond to the following 16 statements:

☐ 1. My spouse and I respect each other's differences.

☐ 2. My spouse and I differ on some major issues but seldom talk about them.

☐ 3. Since my marriage, I have been successful in establishing healthy boundaries with my biological family.

☐ 4. I believe that achieving healthy intimacy with another person is something that happens only to a "lucky" few.

☐ 5. I recognize that healthy intimacy begins with me and can be shared with another person only if I have a clear awareness of, and confidence in, myself.

☐ 6. Sometimes I think I am too dependent upon my spouse.

☐ 7. My spouse is too independent.

☐ 8. I do not trust my spouse in at least one area of major importance to me.

☐ 9. Sometimes I feel like a "single" person who lives a "married life."

☐ 10. I wish I could tell someone how unsatisfactory my marriage is.

☐ 11. I feel my spouse has emotionally withdrawn from me.

☐ 12. My spouse and I are compatible in those areas that are of significant value to me.

☐ 13. I believe that members of the immediate family are being hurt by the poor quality of my marriage.

☐ 14. If I could, I would leave my marriage.

☐ 15. I would like to discover some alternatives that could improve the quality of my marriage.

☐ 16. My spouse would participate in marital counseling.

3

LEGAL AND FINANCIAL
IMPLICATIONS OF DIVORCE

The day of the divorce hearing had arrived. The woman was sitting in the courtroom with her lawyer, anxiously waiting for the procedure to begin. The judge was late. Finally, he appeared. He walked up to the table where the women were sitting, looked at the wife, and said sarcastically, "What's this one over, a microwave oven?"

The joining of two people in marriage and the severing of marriage ties by divorce are intensely personal acts. In them, men and women experience some of life's deepest emotions and most intense interactions.

But marriage and divorce are also public acts, governed by the laws of the state. When a divorce process is initiated, the couple's private relationship is thrust into the public arena. The hurts and disappointments suffered in private are translated into the impersonal and often confusing legal language of petitions, hearings, and public records.

In divorce, the couple's financial assets and obligations also come under scrutiny. Issues like resolving a debt, dividing property, and planning a budget become matters for attorneys' debates and judges' rulings. In a time of increased stress, the divorcing couple must make choices and decisions that will affect their lives for many years.

> The great irony of the divorce process is that although marital separation creates enormous stress and internal turmoil for the couple and other family members, the legal process requires individuals to respond to the crisis rationally and to control powerful feelings. At a time when families experience great vulnerability, society demands that they make decisions and solve problems, maintain self-confidence in the face of rejection, and remain fearless in the face of conflict.[1]

In this chapter we will examine the legal and financial implications of divorce. We will take you step-by-step through the divorce process followed in most states. We will focus on the financial issues a woman should consider before and during a divorce action. In both the legal and financial areas, we will offer cautions and advice from experts to protect your rights and interests.

Knowing what you're likely to face in the attorney's office and the courtroom will remove some of the mystery from the process and, we hope, the anxiety as well.

SEEING THE DIVORCE LAWYER

By the time you or your spouse decides to see a lawyer who handles divorce cases, you have recognized that your marriage has serious problems. Perhaps you've been to a marriage counselor or therapist and have tried to work out your difficulties. You may have discussed your thoughts about divorce and whether it is in your best interest, without actually having initiated divorce proceedings. One or both of you may have decided the marriage cannot be preserved, and you are taking the first step to initiate the divorce process.

However, consulting with an attorney does not necessarily mean you have decided divorce is necessary. Women typically resist contacting an attorney because they may feel they are betraying their spouse. There is a difference between consulting with an attorney and hiring one to represent you in a divorce action. Therapists can help women in this position by referring them to attorneys for consultation and helping them prepare a list of questions about the divorce process and how they will be affected if their marriage is dissolved.

Divorce and family law has become a specialty area. You're likely to find listings of several divorce lawyers in the "Attorneys" section of your yellow pages telephone directory. The local bar association may also be able to provide you with a list of divorce lawyers who practice in your county.

It's important to choose a lawyer who has good negotiating skills and has had experience with divorce cases. You'll want an attorney who is aggressive enough to pursue what is in your best interests. Call several firms to inquire about their experience, their track record, and their rates. You can also ask for referrals from relatives or friends who have used divorce lawyers. But the choice must be yours. It's important that you feel comfortable with the attorney you select, so meet with him or her before you make your choice. (There may be no charge for the first consultation; be sure to ask.) Look for such qualities as intelligence, confidence, patience, and compassion, but don't expect your lawyer to be your therapist or financial advisor. And remember, the lawyer works for you. If you discover later that you made a poor choice, you have the right to fire that attorney and hire another one.

Depending on where you live, hourly fees can range from approximately $75 to $250 or more. Estimates of the cost of handling a typical divorce case range between $1,500 and $5,000, but complex ones that drag on can run higher. Be sure you have a clear understanding of the fees at the outset, including court costs and other expenses, as well as when they are to be paid. The attorney should provide this in writing. Once you retain a lawyer, you will be charged for any and all time he or she spends on your case. This includes consultations, phone calls, reviewing documents, and preparing correspondence. Many law firms employ paralegals to assist attorneys, and their hourly rates will be less for work done on the client's case. Later in this chapter, we'll discuss alternatives to hiring an attorney who charges an hourly fee.

An article in *Working Woman* magazine recommends that a woman manage her divorce as she would a business project, beginning with steps such as the following for choosing and working with a lawyer:[2]

1. Know what to expect. Learn about the divorce laws in your state.
2. Pick an attorney you can work with.
3. Narrow your search to three candidates.
4. Ask about all fees and expenses.
5. Consider arbitration, if available in your state, if you think your divorce will be friendly and you and your spouse are in a fairly equal power relationship.
6. Investigate mediation, which allows parties to reach their own agreement (more on this later).
7. Set limits, clarifying which legal expenses you will be expected to pay and who will do the work.
8. Stay on top of your case, asking questions and keeping a close eye on costs.
9. If you have any doubts, discuss them with your attorney, get a second opinion, and, if necessary, fire your attorney.

In an attempt to save on attorney's fees, some divorcing couples may consider using one lawyer to handle their case. However, this is not recommended. Technically, an attorney can represent only one party in court, and the other party goes into court unrepresented. A lawyer who states that he or she will represent the interests of both parties may be committing malpractice. A woman who relies on her husband's lawyer to look out for her interests will be at a disadvantage. The money saved up front may be eclipsed by losses to the woman in property division and maintenance agreements.

In your first session with the lawyer, you may have a number of questions, such as: How much will this cost? How long will it take? What's going to happen next? What will be expected of me? Don't hesitate to ask such questions. You hire an attorney for his or her professional expertise, but you have a right to know everything related to your case. The lawyer can go over the divorce procedure with you. Divorce codes vary from state to state, and procedures can differ from county to county. But in most cases two conditions must be established before a divorce action can begin.

First, the spouse filing for divorce must establish proof of his or her residence in the county and state in which the papers are filed. Your attorney can explain your state's requirements for length of residency. If one spouse has moved to another locale and has established residency there, filing can be done in either municipality. There may be an advantage to filing in one county if, for example, the court there tends to rule more equitably. This is something you can discuss with your attorney.

Second, the grounds or reasons for the divorce must be determined. Grounds are usually stated in such terms as "incompatibility," "irreconcilable differences," or "irretrievable breakdown of the marriage." The terms mean that the couple cannot continue to live together as husband and wife and the situation is not likely to change in the future.

Virtually all states now allow for such "no-fault" grounds for divorce. This eliminates the necessity of placing blame on one spouse and detailing specific grievances. Before "no-fault," the wronged spouse had to prove misconduct, such as adultery, cruelty, or desertion. With the no-fault procedure, the mudslinging divorce hearings of former times are becoming less common. No-fault divorce protects privacy, shields the children, and promotes a speedier settlement of the case.

However, with the no-fault procedure, the wife is no longer considered the wounded party, as was often the case in the past, and hence is not entitled to special consideration in settlement decisions. Some states allow for the option of fault or no-fault. There may be some advantages to the fault procedure in cases where one spouse has been truly wronged by the gross misconduct of the other. Your attorney can advise you on the best approach if the option exists in your state.

FILING THE DIVORCE ACTION

If you are initiating the divorce action, your attorney prepares and files a summons and a petition at the courthouse. These are legal documents that are necessary to begin the divorce proceeding. The summons establishes legal jurisdiction of the court over your spouse. The petition sets forth the grounds for the divorce, the relief you are seeking, and other requirements. The court system charges a filing fee—usually about one hundred dollars—to process these papers.

In order to inform your spouse of the action, copies of the documents are served on him. This can be done in a number of ways: through the lawyers of both parties, through the mail, by a private process server, or by the sheriff's department. Discuss with your lawyer the best method to use in your situation, as the manner for handling this initial step can set the tone for the whole case.

Divorce can be a painful and unpleasant process. Preserving one's dignity and showing respect for one another throughout the procedure can minimize the trauma. As a courtesy, you may decide to tell your spouse in advance that the papers will be served. The embarrassing scenes of the past, when a sheriff's deputy showed up at the husband's workplace to publicly serve the papers, are rare today.

Seldom does a divorce action come as a complete surprise to the spouse. However, if you anticipate a strong reaction from your spouse and serious consequences, discuss this with your lawyer. If you fear he will react violently, or if he has already threatened or abused you, your lawyer can obtain a temporary restraining order (TRO) from the court. You will have to appear in court to explain the need for the restraining order, which will involve some minimal court costs. The order will restrict your husband's contact with you and your children. If he violates the order, call the police and your attorney. He may be fined or imprisoned.

The spouse on whom the papers are served takes the next step. He has a set period of time—twenty to thirty days, for example—in which to file a response or answer to the petition. At this point he will likely hire a lawyer if he does not already have one. The response, which is filed at the courthouse, states whether or not the spouse agrees with the divorce action and the requests made in the petition. If your husband files and the papers are served on you, your attorney can file a counterclaim.

If you are dependent on your husband for financial support, you may wish to bring a motion for temporary relief between the time of filing and the trial. You may ask for temporary mainte-nance payments for you, temporary child support and custody, continuing insurance for you and the children, and interim court costs and lawyer's fees.

If you and your spouse are considering divorce, you may have wondered if you should be the one to take the first step. With "no-fault" grounds, it actually matters little, strategically, who initiates the divorce action. The one who files the papers pays the initial filing fee and is responsible, with his or her

attorney, for moving the case along. Otherwise, there is no particular advantage or disadvantage to filing the papers or waiting
to have them served on you. However, in a case involving "fault"
grounds, which spouse files may make a strategic difference.
Your lawyer should discuss this and other strategies with you.

Typically, one spouse wants the divorce more than the
other, and he or she initiates the action. Both may acknowledge
that the marriage has problems. But the woman may hesitate to
take the first step if she sees herself at a disadvantage financially
or fears the changes that divorce brings. Talking with a therapist
can help you make that decision.

Timing may be critical here. If you know your marriage is
over but your husband is hesitating to take legal steps, it may be
to your advantage to file. If your husband has a business or other
significant financial assets, he may use delaying tactics to give
him time to hide or sell off his assets, thus depriving you of your
share. When filing for divorce, your attorney can ask the court to
temporarily freeze all marital assets.

THE WAITING PERIOD

Once the initial steps in the divorce process are taken, some
states require a waiting period before the divorce can proceed.
This "cooling down" period, which may be several months, prevents the couple from rushing to divorce. Some states require
that the couple receive marriage counseling during this period.
The state's intent in requiring counseling is to prevent impulsive,
and perhaps unnecessary, divorces.

Either party can request a hearing for the purpose of getting
a temporary order. This order from a judge sets the ground rules
for the waiting period, including how the couple's assets and
debts will be handled and who will have temporary custody of
the children. The order may help preserve the status quo temporarily, before the marriage is dissolved, or it may change the

current legal relations between the parties. It is designed to prevent one party from taking unfair advantage of the other, ensure financial support during the waiting period, and protect the children.

Your attorney may advise such a temporary order, even if relations with your spouse are friendly. Sometimes unexpected conflicts can arise over such trivial issues as how the meat in the freezer is divided up. The attorneys for both parties can negotiate agreement on the temporary order and get approval from the court. There may be some court costs involved in this procedure.

If the couple is determined to proceed with divorce, some states allow a process known as mediation to take place after the papers are filed. Mediation is a cooperative process that helps a couple reach agreement on key issues before appearing in court for the divorce hearing. The process is facilitated by an objective third party, a person skilled in dispute resolution, such as a social worker, psychologist, or lawyer. Agreements reached in mediation are not binding until approved by the judge in court.

Through mediation, issues such as child custody, financial support, and property division may be aired and resolved outside the adversarial courtroom setting. This can help minimize emotional damage to the couple and limit excessive attorneys' fees. The law may require mediation in your state; if it doesn't, the couple may still want to consider mediation, as it can minimize disputes and make for a speedier court proceeding.

If the issue of child custody and placement is not resolved during mediation and becomes a source of conflict, the court may appoint a guardian *ad litem* to represent the children and protect their interests during the divorce action.

One spouse may voluntarily leave the home before or after the papers are filed, or the temporary order may require it. Without such a court order, a spouse cannot be forced to leave the home. Some lawyers advise the couple to remain together during the waiting period as an economy measure, if they can coexist peaceably.

If there are children living at home, the parent who leaves the home and the children may find that he or she is at a disadvantage when custody is decided. Some attorneys advise that a woman never voluntarily leave the house and children, as this may give the impression that she is abandoning her children. If a woman is afraid of her husband and feels she must leave, she should take the children with her. If it's not convenient to stay temporarily with family members or friends, she can call one of the women's shelters that are found in most communities.

A woman can get a restraining order from the court if she shows that her husband is threatening or abusing her. If you find yourself in this situation, talk it over with your attorney and therapist.

At the end of the waiting period, attorneys for both parties confer with the judge at a pretrial conference, which the couple generally attend. If the terms of the divorce have been agreed upon, the case can be settled at this time. Otherwise, a trial date is set and placed on the court calendar. If the couple change their minds about the divorce during this period, the action can be dismissed or the trial suspended.

FINALIZING THE DIVORCE

The average divorce case takes from six months to a year to finalize. The vast majority of cases—more than 90 percent—are settled by agreement between both parties and their attorneys before they reach the courtroom for trial. This means that much of the work in a divorce case is done prior to the final court appearance at which time a judge rules on the terms of the divorce settlement and terminates the legal bonds of marriage.

In a typical divorce, three major issues loom large: property division, children, and financial support. These are the issues attorneys spend the most time trying to negotiate and resolve.

The more agreement that is reached ahead of time on these issues, the speedier and smoother will be the trial. Other issues can arise to complicate the case as well. Trials may take a few hours, a few days, or several weeks. Your attorney will help prepare you for testifying on your behalf at the trial.

Property division. In most marriages, material possessions, other assets, and debts are accumulated. Property may include the house, furnishings, cars, savings, pension plans, business assets, and so on. As the concept of assets has been broadened, even an educational degree may be considered an asset in some states. In that case, a wife may get compensation for a degree she worked to help her husband obtain.

A major issue in divorce is how to divide assets equitably. In some states, marriage is considered an equal partnership, and anything acquired through marital effort can be divided. The laws on division of property vary from state to state, but most require an equitable distribution. Gifts to one spouse, inherited property, or property brought into a marriage may be excluded from division in some states. If business ownership is in the picture, property division is further complicated.

Children. The presence of children in a divorce raises the issues of custody, placement, and visitation rights. The parent who is granted legal custody is responsible for making decisions affecting the child's welfare, including educational and medical decisions. The noncustodial parent is granted visitation rights, which some states now refer to as "periods of physical placement" to elevate the status of the contacts from mere visiting.

Issues regarding the children can create even more discord in a divorce than those having to do with property. Child issues often translate into money issues, as a parent who spends more time with his or her children may be responsible for less child support.

Changing trends in custody decisions have meant more recognition of the father's role as caretaker and co-parent. Nevertheless, despite more gender neutrality in the law, maternal preference still seems to be the norm, except in rare cases where the mother is proven to be unfit. It is estimated that approximately 90 percent of children of divorce remain with their mothers. However, if custody of the children is contested in court and the judge makes the decision, fathers can be awarded custody.

Financial support. Decisions about financial support include money for the children and maintenance for the spouse (formerly called alimony). All states have established guidelines or standards for child support, whereby the noncustodial parent pays support based on his or her income.

Normally, child support is not taxable for the parent receiving it or deductible for the parent paying it. (A tax advisor or the Internal Revenue Service can provide information on the tax consequences of support payments.) The parent who has physical custody of the children takes the dependents' deduction when filing federal income tax, unless the divorce judgment indicates otherwise or the custodial parent agrees to give the other parent the deduction and signs a tax form so indicating. The court can order that either parent claim the children as dependents on his or her tax return.

Guidelines for spousal maintenance are usually not as clear-cut, although most states have adopted equitable distribution laws in which each spouse gets a fair share of marital assets. Equalization of husband-wife income in a long-term marriage may also be a goal; however, in practice, such equalization rarely happens, and the woman is likely to be the loser financially.

Much has been written in recent years about the changes in economic status that divorced women experience, and a number of studies has shown that these women typically suffer a decline in income and a lower standard of living immediately following marital breakup. Their ex-husbands, on the other hand, often enjoy an increase, widening the disparities in economic well-being between divorced women and men. Lenore J. Weitzman's study of men and women in Los Angeles County found that, on average, the standard of living of women and their minor children declined 73 percent in the first year following divorce, while their former husbands' standard of living rose 42 percent.[3]

Other studies have found the drop to be significant, though not as dramatic. For example, researchers Saul D. Hoffman and Greg J. Duncan reported in 1988 that the decline in economic status (income divided by needs) for the divorced woman is about one-third in the first year.[4] Such economic changes are not surprising, considering that divorced women with children usually carry a larger share of the cost of raising them and a smaller share of the marriage's wealth and earning power.

In *Women, Work, and Divorce*, Richard R. Peterson examined the economic survival of divorced women and their employment patterns. He found that, compared to married women, divorced women have a lower standard of living and higher poverty rates. However, those who worked during marriage fared better after divorce than did those who had not established themselves in the work force while married.[5]

Since marriage is, in effect, a partnership, the employed spouse (usually the husband) benefits from the nonmonetary contributions of the nonemployed spouse (typically the wife). Therefore, advocates for a more equitable treatment of women in divorce settlements maintain that economic arrangements after divorce should aim to equalize the standards of living of both postdivorce households. Susan Moller Okin argues that, in the case of long-term marriages, equalization should continue permanently. She points out that because of the traditional division of labor in the family, the husband usually is able to develop his earning capacity to a greater extent than is his wife. Okin maintains that most displaced homemakers aged forty-five or more "have very little chance of earning more than a small fraction of what their ex-spouses can earn," and that legal and policy changes should address this discrepancy:

> Change must begin with the recognition that future earning power is the principal asset of most marriages. Fewer than 50 percent of divorcing couples have any tangible assets at all, once debt is taken into account. . . . Future earning power, as a crucial asset of a marriage, must be fairly distributed in the event of divorce.[6]

Whether a wife receives maintenance and how much is determined by the judge. Factors that may be taken into consideration include the length of the marriage, the couple's lifestyle, the education and earning capacity of each spouse, and their assets and liabilities. The issue of maintenance is often the area of greatest litigation and the last to be resolved in a divorce case. A husband may threaten a custody battle for the children if he believes his wife is asking for too much spousal support. A husband who is paying maintenance to his ex-wife may resent what he considers to be frivolous expenditures on her part. To avoid further conflict and resentment, the woman should be judicious about how she spends money and avoid purchases that could be viewed as extravagant.

If a wife is not employed, she is usually expected to find a job after the divorce. Her earning potential will be taken into consideration when maintenance is determined. If a woman is capable of supporting herself at the same lifestyle she enjoyed during marriage, she may receive no maintenance payments. If her earning power is greater than her husband's, she may be required to pay support to him.

The decision on the amount of maintenance is not necessarily permanent. It is usually time-limited and subject to review and renewal. Payment increases are not automatic and require a request to the court. However, if the decision on maintenance is closed at the time of divorce finalization, the issue cannot be reopened. If a woman remarries, support from her former spouse ends unless the parties have an agreement to continue spousal support and their state holds such agreements to be legally enforceable.

WHAT ABOUT SEPARATION?

A couple uncertain about the option of divorce may choose a period of trial separation. A nonlegal separation can be entered into at any time and usually means one spouse moves out of the home voluntarily. (However, the wife should be aware that if children are present in the home and she leaves, this could jeopardize her position in a custody conflict.)

In a voluntary separation, the husband and wife may work out the terms themselves or may seek legal counsel. This can be a healthy arrangement that may diffuse the conflict and lead to reconciliation, especially if the couple are working with a counselor or therapist to address their problems.

Legal separation is another option, although it is not common. It may be chosen in situations in which one or both spouses are opposed to divorce on religious grounds. Or it may be a compromise arrived at in the hope that things will get better and make divorce unnecessary.

The procedure and court costs for legal separation are similar to those of divorce, up to the point of the final hearing that terminates the marriage. That is, papers are filed and a temporary order can be sought establishing support and other ground rules. After six months to a year of legal separation, one or both parties may request that the action be converted to a divorce. In most cases, legal separation eventually results in divorce.

ALTERNATIVES TO DIVORCE LAWYERS

You are not required by law to use a lawyer in a divorce proceeding. Some people choose the option of *pro se* divorce in order to save money or because they prefer to handle the case themselves. *Pro se* is a Latin term meaning "for self" and refers to the action of appearing in one's own behalf in a court of law.

Information and resources are available for those who want to pursue *pro se* divorce. You can start by checking your library and local women's center. Many communities have organizations to help you if you choose this route, providing how-to material and other support. These organizations may charge a membership fee, which would be in addition to your filing fee and other costs. Depending on where you live, a *pro se* divorce may cost less than five hundred dollars. This is considerably less than you would pay an attorney who charges hourly fees, which could result in a bill of thousands of dollars.

Pro se divorce may work well for the couple who hasn't been married very long, who are in agreement on property and support issues, and who are seeking similar goals through the divorce. A mediator can help smooth the process in a *pro se* divorce. But those who find themselves in bitter battles over children and property, who have complicated finances, or who are embroiled in emotional battles may have difficulty being objective and rational and will likely need attorney representation.

Another option is to turn to a law firm or family law center that charges flat fees for divorce cases. Check your phone directory yellow pages, and make a few calls to determine fees and what is included.

If you have insufficient income or assets to pay for an attorney, and your husband is in a better economic position, the court may require him to cover the cost of your legal counsel. This assures you of legal representation.

The low-income or indigent woman can turn to the local legal aid services and programs available in most communities. These programs are funded either by federal aid, through United Way contributions, or through other grants. However, resources are scarce and demands are many for these types of services for people who can't afford to pay.

Local agencies set their own priorities for providing help in family matters, which might include domestic violence, custody disputes, and income maintenance. If the requests are many, an agency may take on the most critical ones and maintain a waiting list for others. Nevertheless, if you can't afford to pay for legal help, call your local legal services agency. If they are unable to represent you, they may be able to give helpful advice.

FINANCIAL CONSIDERATIONS

As we have observed, divorce can have devastating economic consequences for women. While rarely does either spouse "win" in a divorce, the woman often comes out with the short end of the financial stick. If you are unemployed or underemployed and have no financial assets of your own, you may find yourself with little control over your economic situation. But there are steps you can take to protect yourself before you divorce and eliminate some of the vulnerability you feel.

The first and perhaps the most important factor is information. How much do you know about the financial condition of your marriage partnership?

In general, women are just as capable as men at managing money. But all too often women turn over family financial matters to their husbands. A wife may not know her husband's annual salary, what's in the savings or retirement accounts, the size of the mortgage, or the couple's total debts. She may know nothing about the value of his pension plan or insurance policies. She may have no idea how much it takes to run the household for a month. She may not have access to the checking account.

This lack of knowledge can put a woman at a disadvantage when she has to manage on her own during and after a divorce. It also makes it easier for a husband, concerned about the financial consequences of divorce, to put aside money in a hidden bank account without his wife's knowledge. We don't like to suspect the worst of those we have loved and trusted, but such things do happen.

A certified public accountant who has worked with divorce lawyers makes the following recommendations to women facing divorce:

1. If you intend to file for divorce or suspect your husband will do so, get copies of all financial records before any action is taken. This should include bank statements, income tax returns for several years, loan papers, credit card debts, stock certificates, brokers' statements, pension and profit sharing plans, and any other records that document your family's financial situation. The key question you are seeking to answer is: How much money is coming in and where is it going? Once the divorce is in process, the records can be subpoenaed to the court. Normally, your attorney will prepare the subpoena.

2. Consider any assets and personal property you may have that were gifts or inheritances made to you alone, or property brought into the marriage. You will need documentation to prove that these were not acquired as part of the marriage. Depending on your state's community property laws, these assets may or may not have to be considered in property division.

3. If you don't know exactly what it takes to run your household monthly, become familiar with your family's routine expenses, such as food, mortgage, utilities, transportation and so on.

4. Begin to develop a budget for yourself that includes personal, household, and child support expenses and, if possible, test it out for several months. Include an extra cushion for unanticipated expenses. This budget will be useful when decisions are negotiated about child support and spousal maintenance.

5. If you do not have a checking or savings account in your own name, open one. In the event that your spouse suddenly

withholds funds, the checking account will give you access to cash for living expenses and fees connected with the divorce. You will have to disclose this asset during the divorce proceeding, but you should be able to retain control over the account.

6. Don't be influenced to sign any legal documents without the advice of your attorney. For example, don't sign any papers that sell or transfer assets, such as stock certificates.

YOUR FINANCIAL FUTURE

During the divorce procedure, your lawyer may recommend the services of a certified public accountant (CPA) to help assess the current value and income potential of real estate, a business, or other assets owned by the couple. The CPA will make recommendations about property division and compensation that should increase your chances of getting an equitable settlement. It could be a costly mistake for you to accept the first compensation offer from your spouse, which may underestimate the future value of those assets.

A good CPA can also examine the tax consequences of any settlement you receive as a result of the divorce and can recommend arrangements that will work to your advantage. If you are not aware of the tax rules, you could lose money. For example, since you will have to pay income tax on the support payments you receive, a $500 a week payment from your ex-husband could turn out to be much less after taxes.

If a CPA is employed to work on your case, you will most likely be billed directly for these services. You can inquire about fees beforehand, which range from about $75 to $150 an hour in most parts of the country.

If you have never done financial planning, a divorce is certainly a crucial time to ponder your financial future and take steps to protect it. Planning includes consideration of your cash flow needs in the near future and in retirement, your income potential, and the nature of any savings and investments you will make.

Independent financial planners and investment counselors can help you evaluate your situation and make such decisions. You can ask your attorney or CPA to recommend someone who is credible and reliable. Check on several, interview them and ask for references. Also ask if they receive commissions for recommending certain investments. Take this step before you've spent that lump sum you may receive in a divorce settlement.

Navigating your way through the complex legal and financial aspects of divorce certainly isn't easy. If you're entering the turbulent waters of divorce action, it's essential that you do so with your eyes wide open and as much knowledge as you can acquire. Know what you're entitled to, and take every step you can to protect yourself and your children—physically, emotionally, and financially. Make use of professionals with the expertise to help you, even if it means spending extra dollars now. You're likely to come out better in the long run.

CHECKLIST

The checklist that follows is a brief summary of the basic procedures and recommendations discussed in this chapter. The list assumes that the decision to divorce has already been made and that you and your spouse have sought counseling and made every effort to improve your relationship.

☐ 1. Make a list of divorce lawyers who practice in your county and select several to call.

☐ 2. Interview several attorneys and select an experienced one with whom you feel comfortable.

☐ 3. Inquire about fees and expenses and get written retainer agreements.

☐ 4. Ask your attorney to explain your state's divorce code and the procedures that will be followed.

☐ 5. Get copies of all your family's financial records before filing for divorce.

☐ 6. Develop a personal and household budget if you do not have one.

☐ 7. Open a checking or savings account in your own name if you don't have one.

☐ 8. If your spouse has not filed for divorce, discuss with your attorney if and when you should take this step.

☐   9. If your spouse has filed, discuss with your attorney the response and counterclaim.

☐ 10. Don't sign any legal or financial documents without your attorney's advice.

☐ 11. Determine with your attorney if you need a preliminary court hearing and temporary order while you wait for the divorce to be finalized.

☐ 12. Inquire about mediation: Is it required in your state? Would it be helpful?

☐ 13. Consult with a certified public accountant for help determining assets and getting an equitable settlement.

☐ 14. Work with your attorney to arrive at the terms of the divorce settlement.

☐ 15. If your case isn't settled prior to the trial, work with your attorney in preparing for your testimony in court.

☐ 16. Undertake long-range financial planning to ensure your future security

4

WOMEN AND DEPRESSION

I am a woman. I am depressed.
I learned this way of responding to life
From my mother who learned it from her mother.

I am a woman. I am depressed.
I learned from my culture that a woman
should not express anger.
(When she does, she's called a nag, witch, or bitch.)
Therefore, I internalize and repress anger.

I am a woman. I am depressed.
As a woman, I am supposed to be
the reconciler and harmonizer.
So, if there's conflict, it's my fault because I
should be able to prevent it or cure it singlehandedly.

I am a woman. I am depressed.
I expect perfection of myself
so I'm harshly critical of myself
for real or imagined shortcomings.
If anything is wrong anywhere or with anyone,
it is somehow my fault and/or my responsibility to fix it.
If I don't or can't, there is something wrong with me.

I am a woman. I am depressed.
I learned to "love my neighbor" more than myself.
I have become depleted, drained, empty because I haven't
refueled as I've given out. I "don't have time" for me.

I am a woman. I am depressed.
To care for me as much as my neighbor would be selfish.
I keep my needs and wants to myself,
hoping someone will notice and "be sensitive to me"
as I am to others. I feel resentful that I give so much
and get so little.

I am a woman. I am depressed.
I am externally focused: On pleasing others.
(I don't know what pleases me);
On seeking others' approval.
(I don't give myself approval);
On adapting to others' needs and expectations.
(I don't know what I need or expect);
On affirming others.
(I wouldn't think of buying myself roses
or writing myself a thank you note.)

I am a woman. I deserve to feel good.
I deserve to love myself as my neighbor.
In fact, this is Jesus' command.
Love your neighbor as yourself
reverses to love yourself as your neighbor.

I am a woman.
I have a right to know when I am angry,
to feel the anger and to choose
to appropriately express it.

I am a woman.
I have a right to make mistakes
and to put my energy into doing better
when I know how or what to do better
(rather than whipping myself with guilt and recrimination).

I am a woman.
I have a right and duty to nurture myself
and the child within me, to re mother
the hurt, sad, fearful and angry child within me;
to give this self the unconditional love
for which she's been waiting so long.

Dr. Sharron K. St. John
Reprinted by permission of the author[1]

The lament of the universal woman in the lines above may strike a familiar chord with many of us. As women, we are particularly susceptible to depression if we are in troubled marriages or are separated or divorced. In fact, a major study has shown that women are twice as likely as men to experience depression. Particularly noteworthy were the findings that women are three times more likely than men to be depressed in unhappy marriages, and almost half of all women in unhappy marriages are depressed.[2]

The relationship between marital status and depression also suggests:

- Separated and divorced persons revealed the highest rate of depressive symptoms, and those never-married and presently married showed the lowest

- Rates were found to be lower among married people than among single people

- One's sex and marital status play a part in depression.

When ranked from lowest to highest, depression rates oc-curred in groups in the following order:

1) Married men (lowest rate)
2) Married women
3) Single and widowed women
4) Single, widowed, and divorced men
5) Separated and divorced women (highest rate)[3]

This suggests that separated and divorced women are at the highest level of risk for one of our nation's most serious health problems.

All of us have experienced feelings of sadness from time to time. We see a dejected child sitting idly by while other children exclude the youngster from their games, and we feel sad. We experience the loss of a close relationship, and we feel de-pressed. We experience the death of a loved one, and we feel a deep sense of grief. Complaints of sadness, depression, and grief under such circumstances are normal, expected, and predictable. The pain and suffering are very real. However, unlike depression that requires treatment, this "blue" feeling allows the sufferer to continue to function adequately without treatment and, in time, the symptoms begin to subside and the mood lifts.

Clinical depression, on the other hand, is the general term applied to a number of depressions in which the duration and intensity of symptoms are severe enough to require treatment because the sufferer is unable to function effectively in daily life. Though several forms of clinical depression exist, this chapter will focus on major depression, one of the prevalent forms that women suffer. While a number of factors can set off major depression, a stressful life event is often a precipitating factor. Events involving loss are particularly prone to lead to a depres-sive illness. And loss by divorce—regardless of whether the in-dividual is the plaintiff or the defendant, and irrespective of whether the divorce is a mutual decision or a cataclysmic battle —is a high-risk stressor, capable of producing a serious major depression.

As a recently divorced woman attempts to adapt to her new multiple role responsibilities, the increased stress she faces can exacerbate the symptoms of major depression. For example, it is not uncommon for a woman to feel overwhelmed when she must assume the role of full-time wage earner and custodial parent of the children, as well as take on new tasks that may be completely unfamiliar to her. Pressure resulting from the enormous demands placed upon her can add to the stress she already feels, and her feelings of inadequacy and hopelessness about the future— symptoms commonly associated with major depression—can intensify. The older woman who divorces after many years of marriage, and whose older children may have not yet left the home, can feel equally stressed as she finds herself sandwiched between the needs of her offspring and her aging parents.

Clinical depression can be life-threatening, as individuals who suffer from it are at high risk for suicide. Long-term, follow-up studies have found a 15 percent suicide rate in persons with serious clinical depressions that are not associated with other psychiatric disorders. Although men are three to four times more likely to take their own lives than are women, women attempt suicide three to four times more frequently than men. These differences in suicide rates between the sexes can be linked to the methods chosen to commit suicide: Males choose more active methods like shooting themselves, while females choose more passive methods like ingesting toxic substances, such as sleeping pills, which often do not cause immediate death. Firearms are the preferred method for those individuals with high suicidal intent, since survival is rare when guns are used.

One can gain insight into the logic of the potentially suicidal person by recognizing that the tendency toward suicide is governed by the application of a simple formula: the ratio between a person's fear of life and fear of death. For most people, the fear of death is greater than the fear of life. However, for the suicidal person, the fear of life has become greater than the fear of death. For them, life has become so filled with intolerable pain, hopelessness, and helplessness, that the alternative of death seems comforting.

Therefore, as individuals begin to experience symptoms of serious clinical depression, it is important for them to seek the help needed to increase the ratio in favor of life. Lessening the potential for suicide will rest to a large extent upon their ability to decrease their fear of life and increase its gratifications.

A final word about the relationship between suicide and depression: Some experts estimate that as many as 75,000 people may commit suicide each year. And though prediction of suicide is not always possible, it is clear that about three quarters of the people who kill themselves are depressed at the time.[4] In addition, 80 percent of those who complete suicides have communicated their intent to others prior to committing the act.[5] They aren't merely crying out for help when they communicate their intention toward self-destruction. These people frequently do die, and their warning messages must be taken seriously.

Some women recognize the signs of major depression and seek medical help to alleviate the symptoms, as well as the underlying causes of those symptoms. There are others, however, who, at enormous cost, choose not to recognize, accept, and confront their depression. As Dr. St. John's insightful words at the beginning of this chapter suggest, women's perfectionism, repressed anger, guilt, self-reproach, and need to please and adapt to others all can become deterrents to focusing on one's own emotional needs. Hence, a woman who embraces the traditional feminine urge to anticipate, identify, and respond first to the needs of others in her life may neglect her own self-nurturing. And, over time, as the self is left unnurtured, physiological and psychological symptoms can develop. Ironically, her increased fatigue, indecisiveness, and other depressive symptoms can then prevent her from seeking the very medical advice and/or treatment she needs.

Regardless of age, socioeconomic class, or race and culture, millions of people in our country suffer from depressive disorders. And, though almost 80 percent of all serious depressions can be successfully treated, relatively few victims seek help. Consequently, people suffer needlessly for months and sometimes years from the debilitating effects of clinical depression.

Though the next chapter will discuss the expected and predictable signs of short-term depression that are associated with the grief process, we will devote the remainder of this chapter to the characteristic signs of major depression, its primary causes, and information for those who may seek treatment.

THE SIGNS OF MAJOR DEPRESSION

Major depression is one form of clinical depression. To be diagnosed as such, its symptoms must meet specific criteria for duration, functional impairment, and involvement of a cluster of both physiological and psychological symptoms. This disorder, therefore, is an illness with distinct and explicit symptoms, which can seriously affect our overall functioning. The following case study illustrates the symptoms of a divorced woman suffering from major depression.

The Case of Carolyn

Carolyn, an attractive, articulate, but despondent thirty-five-year-old woman, leaned forward on the couch in the therapist's office, staring at the rug below her feet. Her fists were clenched and her arms were wrapped around her stomach, indicating her anger and her unconscious need to "hold herself together." Her voice shook as she glanced quickly at the therapist and said tearfully, "I feel completely out of control." It was Carolyn's first visit to her therapist's office, and during the next several minutes she told the following story:

"I was twenty-two years old when I married Brian, my college sweetheart. We both decided that we didn't want children because we had our careers to develop. We had a good life together until about a year and a half ago, when it became clear to both of us that our lives were going in different directions. His schedule didn't correspond with mine, and we no longer found time just for each other. He went his way and I went mine and things went from bad to worse.

"We didn't talk about it much, but we both knew that each of us was pretty miserable, so we finally decided to separate. That was a year ago. He served me with papers about one month later and our divorce became final about four months ago. At the time of our separation, I was certain that I could handle being single because my family was very supportive and I had always been self-confident and resourceful. But things didn't go like I thought they would.

"When my husband left, it seemed like all my friends did, too. I now realize why: My only friends were my husband's friends. And my social life was filled with couples' activities. We played golf in couples. We went to dinner in couples. We went to concerts in couples. We even went on vacations in couples. I didn't even know a woman who was separated or divorced!

"One of the things that really struck me as strange was this: Soon after our divorce, I learned through the grapevine that wives of couples my husband and I had known for years began to invite him to dinner. They never once invited me to dinner! I wondered if my presence as a single woman at their dinner table might somehow intimidate my former female friends. I also wondered if they thought Brian lacked the wherewithal to make a home-cooked meal for himself. Little did they know that he probably was eating better than I was. I couldn't eat at restaurants by myself because I felt so lonely. And I didn't want to take time to cook for myself when I got home from work, so I would stand alone in my kitchen and eat junk food. The only comfort I could find around me was in the food I would inhale. I've gained twenty pounds since my divorce became final!

"About two months ago, I began to feel very depressed, so I threw myself into my work and spent longer days at the office. I began to feel like a clam who was shut up in solitary confinement. And true to my mollusk-like existence, I finally recognized I was attached to that outer shell because I had lost my backbone. I came out only to go to work and to shovel in chocolate ice cream at night.

"And then my boss tried to help. He called me into his office and in a gentle way tried to tell me he was becoming concerned about my work. He said I had missed some important details in one of the business contracts that I had negotiated. I told him the mistake was probably the result of the late nights I had been keeping, and explained that I would try to get more rest. What I didn't tell him was that I was getting into an awful routine: As soon as I would get home from work, I would devour some fast food, nod off on the living room sofa, wake up two hours later, and pace through the house like a caged panther for most of the rest of the night.

"After my boss talked with me, I knew my problem was getting serious enough to require a change in my life. I thought if I could get more exercise I might sleep better, so I paid a lot of money to join a tennis club. I used to love to play tennis, and I was pretty good at it, too. But I haven't played once since I joined.

"The whole problem is so stupid. I'm really angry with myself. I should be able to handle this on my own. I manage millions of dollars of other people's money every year, and I can't even manage my own life! I wish I could change what is happening to me, but I can't. I don't want to keep feeling so rotten all the time. It would be such a relief if God would just let me go to sleep and not bother to ever wake me up."

The onset of Carolyn's major depression was rooted in the early stages of her marital dissolution. Though the severity, range, and duration of symptoms of this form of clinical depression vary, she suffered from nearly all of the common signs of this disorder. Symptoms of major depression, which can have a serious adverse effect on our feelings, thoughts, and behaviors, include:

- A persistent sad, anxious or "empty" mood

- Feelings of hopelessness, pessimism

- Feelings of guilt, worthlessness, helplessness

- Loss of interest or pleasure in activities that you once enjoyed, including sex

- Sleep disturbances (insomnia, early-morning awakening, or oversleeping)

- Eating disturbances (changes in appetite and/or weight loss or weight gain)

- Decreased energy, fatigue, being "slowed down"

- Thoughts of death or suicide or suicide attempts

- Restlessness, irritability

- Difficulty concentrating, remembering, making decisions

A depressed person may experience any or all of these symptoms. However, the likelihood of being diagnosed with major depression is significantly increased if symptoms of sadness and hopelessness, as well as a loss of pleasure in activities she previously enjoyed, have been ongoing and interfere with her functioning. In addition, suicidal thoughts, whether passive—"I wish I would not wake up in the morning"—or active—"I have a definite plan in mind for destroying myself"—are particular cause for concern. They may indicate that an individual is acutely depressed and in need of treatment.

Early diagnosis can often prevent the development of more severe psychological problems that interfere with a sufferer's ability to function. For example, if left untreated, major depression can lead to delusional and hallucinatory symptoms, as well as disturbances of the higher mental functions of thought, perception, and orientation.

While the symptoms listed above are those commonly associated with major depression, when a woman seeks treatment, her condition is diagnosed on the basis of criteria contained in the *Diagnostic and Statistical Manual of Mental Disorders*, Fourth Edition (DSM-IV).[6] The criteria designated in the 1994 DSM-IV are found in the checklist at the end of this chapter.

It is important to keep in mind that the process of diagnosis of major depression involves the evaluation of a number of factors. Because diagnosis is complicated, an accurate assessment requires the expertise of an experienced health care professional.

When women like Carolyn pursue therapy, they often say they feel "out-of-control." This is a condition of perceived helplessness—a seemingly impenetrable, self-defeating, "chicken and egg" predicament: "Because I feel out-of-control (helpless), I prevent myself from doing things that I know would be healthy for me; and because I am unable to do things that I know would be healthy for me, I continue to feel "out-of-control (helpless)." This dilemma—in which one's perceived helplessness fosters self-defeating behavior that, in turn, intensifies perceptions of helplessness—is one of the major dynamics that can set the stage for major depression.

Like so many others who suffer the effects of major depression, Carolyn's statement, "I wish I could change what is happening to me, but I can't," shows how she perceives her predicament. But for most depressed women, the remark "I can't change" really means "I don't know how to change" or "I am terrified to attempt change."

Furthermore, her statement, "I wish I could change what is happening to me," shows that she sees the environment as acting upon her. While there are, indeed, some conditions over which we have little control, we render ourselves impotent if we believe we have no control at all and things just happen to us.

Carolyn presents herself as a hopeless, vulnerable, resourceless woman who believes she can't change, among other things: (a) her feelings of abandonment by her previous friendship circle, (b) unhealthy eating habits, (c) poor sleeping patterns, (d) a life that seems devoid of pleasure or gratification, (e) her workaholism (which, ironically, appears to be one of the few ways in which Carolyn can escape from her feelings of helplessness), and (f) her feelings of loneliness. In short, Carolyn has become paralyzed by a self-imposed loss of will, which is deeply rooted in her belief that she lacks the ability to cope and exert control over the outcomes she desires in her life. This paralysis severely restricted her ability to develop and commit to goals—even those that she knew would have a healthy effect on her.

Not surprisingly, the opposite of helplessness is controllability, which can retrieve us from depression. Therefore, one of the key goals of treatment for a clinically depressed woman is to break the "chicken and egg" cycle by helping her regain the belief that she can exert control over many of the valued outcomes in her life. A few of the strategies that can increase a woman's feelings of hope, pleasure, and vitality, and help her reestablish a sense of control over her life, are found at the conclusion of Chapter Five.

THE CAUSES OF MAJOR DEPRESSION

Though some people who suffer from major depression experience only one serious episode in their lifetime, for many others the condition resurfaces, often with recurring episodes. Each episode may be separated by a long interval, sometimes lasting years. On the other hand, the episodes may be close together and may even appear to cluster. If left untreated, episodes of major depression usually last about one year.

But what causes this debilitating disorder that now affects an astonishing seven million women in our society? There is no simple answer to this question, because today we know that the risk factors that contribute to clinical depression are many and complex and that they interact. The following discussion focuses on some of these factors that can create vulnerability to depression. Much of the information is derived from the valuable research and numerous publications produced by the U. S. Department of Health and Human Services' National Institute of Mental Health.

Genetic Factors. It is difficult to determine the extent to which clinical depression may be linked to either heredity or the environment in which we live. However, studies of identical twins have provided considerable evidence that a genetic factor is somehow involved in the transmission of depressive disorders. Identical twins come from the same fertilized egg and, therefore, have the same genetic makeup, while fraternal twins (and other siblings) come from two different eggs and share only 50 percent of their genes in common.

One important study, conducted in Denmark in 1979, suggests that if one identical twin develops depression or mania (commonly found in bipolar disorder, formerly known as manic-depressive disorder), the other twin has a 70 percent chance of developing the disorder as well. A nonidentical (fraternal) twin or first-degree relative (such as a parent or sibling) of a depression or mania sufferer has a 15 percent chance of developing the disorder. Among second-degree relatives (such as cousins or grandparents), who share even less than one-half of the gene pool in common, the risk is about seven percent.

Other research exploring the role of genetics in depression has been conducted with adopted individuals diagnosed as having a depressive disorder. One study compared the incidence of diagnosed depression in biological and adoptive parents and their children. Higher correlations were found between depressed adoptees, particularly those suffering from bipolar disorder, and their biological parents than with the adoptive parents who had raised them from early childhood.

Also suggestive of a genetic link was the finding in the Denmark study that the concentration of depression among biological relatives is three times greater than that found among adopting families.

The discerning reader might wonder why the identical twin of one individual suffering from major depression or bipolar disorder would have only a 70 percent chance, rather than a 100 percent chance, of developing a depressive illness. Identical twins do, after all, share all of their genes in common. One explanation may be that the genes may create a vulnerability to these disorders, with other factors contributing to the actual onset of the disease. For example, many researchers believe that the family environment predisposes people to maladaptive ways of thinking, feeling, and behaving. Still others suggest depression may be attributable to biochemical influences that create a vulnerability to depression. Hence, separating the genetic, biological, and environmental factors associated with depression is a complex undertaking and one that requires far more research.

Biochemical Factors. A neuron, or nerve cell, of which there are more than 100 billion in the human brain, is the basic unit for transmitting brain messages by means of electrical impulses. Because nerve cells themselves do not touch each other directly, and each is separated by a tiny space called a synapse, chemical substances called "neurotransmitters" send electrochemical signals from one nerve cell in the brain to another. More than 50 different neurotransmitters, each with unique chemical properties, have been discovered.

Research has suggested that either depletion, abundance, or an improper balance of neurotransmitters in the brain is related to episodes of depression and mania. An imbalance, particularly a deficiency, in two of the brain's neurotransmitters—serotonin and norepinephrine—has been linked to depression. Excessive norepinephrine has been associated with highly agitated, manic states. At least two other neurotransmitters, dopamine and acetylcholine, have been associated with depression. Electrolytes and hormones, substances involved in neurotransmission, are also being investigated for their involvement. Researchers suspect that the different types of depressive disorders may be based on a series of dysfunctions related to the firing of specific chains or combinations of chains of neurons.

For now, we can only speculate about the biological stimuli that may be associated with the onset of a particular type of clinical depression. And, as science continues to put together the complicated pieces of the depression puzzle, we may find that the neurotransmitters are merely links in a long and complex chain of reactions that affect human mood and emotion. As the mystery unfolds, it may shed light on whether physical and mood changes associated with depressive disturbances are caused by biochemical factors, or whether physical and mood changes cause the biochemical disturbances.

OTHER FACTORS ASSOCIATED WITH CLINICAL DEPRESSION

Environmental Stressors. We have seen that the stresses facing women in contemporary society can predispose them to depression. Four "vulnerability factors" have been identified that appear to increase the likelihood that a woman will experience a depressive episode in the face of a stressful life event: unemployment, three or more children under the age of fourteen at home, lack of a confiding relationship with a partner, and childhood loss of a parent through death or separation.[7] Each of these four factors appears to contribute to depression by rendering an individual less able to cope with stress.

One particular parenting situation that is common in our country appears to be a precursor to clinical depression in women. It has been estimated that between 1.35 and 2.25 million children in the United States suffer from Attention Deficit Disorder (ADD). These children are prone to have other problems as well, such as difficulties with learning, behavior, and social or emotional development. Experts suggest that 40 percent of mothers with hyperactive children suffer from depression as they try to cope with, and effectively handle, the many frustrations and demands of parenting an ADD child.[8] The divorced woman who must raise such a child on her own faces a formidable challenge indeed.

In the wake of divorce, many women are also forced to confront other life stressors alone. For example, during and following marital dissolution, women often face, singlehandedly, financial problems, legal disputes, dramatic changes in lifestyle, childrearing as a single parent, children leaving home, and job changes. And, if any of these life events is sufficiently threatening, the susceptibility to clinical depression is increased for those women who have trouble adapting.

It is clear that environmental stressors can cause, or interact with, vulnerability factors that create a predisposition to clinical depression. However, clinical depression can also cause stressful consequences. For example, women who are clinically depressed often submerge themselves in self-defeating self-talk about feelings of worthlessness and hopelessness. They also blame themselves for their inability to change themselves or the stressful situations associated with their depression.

Furthermore, clinically depressed people generally do not exhibit a "self-serving bias." This bias is the universal tendency of nondepressed people to attribute results to internal factors when the consequences are positive but to external factors when the consequences are negative. For example, a person might say, "I earned a 10 percent salary increase last year because I accomplished my work goals efficiently and competently" (an internal attribution), but say, "My boss gave me only a two percent salary increase this year because he's a stingy person" (an external attribution).

On the other hand, depressed people often subscribe to the reverse of the "self-serving bias," attributing success to external factors while blaming themselves for their failures. Furthermore, there is evidence that women in general—not just those who are depressed—are more likely to attribute their success to external, unstable factors such as luck, while men most often credit their success to internal, stable factors such as intelligence or ability. If women attribute positive outcomes to external factors, they begin to think:

> . . . that their lives are externally controlled only when it comes to success. When they fail, they suddenly turn internal, blaming their poor showing on a lack of ability. These women are caught: if they do well, they sacrifice the credit, but if they bomb, they shoulder the blame. Sooner or later a woman in this situation is likely to decide that if at first she doesn't succeed, she might as well forget it.[9]

As depressed people continue to victimize themselves through their self-deprecating thought processes ("I'm not OK, the world's not OK, and there's nothing I can do about it"), they often respond to their own discomfort by seeking sympathy from others. However, while depressive behavior may initially elicit sympathy and attention, the response from friends and relatives generally is short-lived and replaced by other less empathic responses. As one articulate woman observed: "I began to play the 'depression game,' and it resulted in my getting the reverse of what I was looking for. My husband and kids became 'burned out' trying to attend to my need for nurturing. And they began to suspect that my depression was a manipulative ploy to receive attention and sympathy, so they became distrustful of me and began to withdraw from me."

And, as others begin to withdraw, the clinically depressed woman is unable to fulfill unmet needs, which often leads her into a condition of self-imposed solitary confinement. Unfortunately, as depressed people disengage from others, they isolate themselves from those who are capable of both providing positive reinforcement and satisfying the basic human need for belonging. And as the detachment worsens, the downward spiral of depression gains momentum.

From another perspective, there appears to be a relationship between social detachment and depression in our society. Americans place a premium on individualism, sometimes at the expense of connectedness to others. This independent streak is not without cost. Taken too far, a preoccupation with the self can result in social detachment, which can lead to depression. Though independence is a valued human quality, narcissistic independence, which may result in the lack of interest or inability to gain a sense of social interdependence, can seriously impair our need to feel interconnected with humankind. This condition can chip away at the human spirit and generate a state of profound loneliness.

America's highly technological society requires us to work harder at preventing the potential consequences of individualism, independence, depersonalization, and isolation. John Naisbitt argued in his national best seller *Megatrends* that Americans must learn to balance the material wonders of technology with the spiritual demands of their human nature.[10] As Naisbitt speculated, "human touch" is essential in a highly technological society, and some technology, no matter how advanced, will never be able to replace the need for human contact. Though his book was written more than a decade ago, his prophetic insights have withstood the test of time. As yet, teleconferencing has not replaced face-to-face meetings, high-tech delivery rooms have not replaced low-tech birthing rooms, home videos have not replaced theaters, electronic shopping has not replaced food markets, and electronic funds transfers have not replaced bank tellers.

Health and Physical Illness. Though the causal relationship of depression and bodily functions is still largely misunderstood, it is well-known that clinical depression is frequently connected to physical illnesses. For example, people suffering from Huntington's Chorea, Parkinson's disease, or stroke, suffer from depression produced by the disease itself, which causes injury to, or malfunction of, nerves within the brain.

Moreover, though not all clinical depression is caused by physical illnesses, the two conditions are often found together. For example, mononucleosis, rheumatic fever, anemia, ulcerative colitis, and asthma are among the many illnesses in a long list of physical conditions that are associated with depression. Depression is also linked to other psychiatric disorders, including alcoholism, substance abuse, eating disorders, and anxiety disorders.

In addition, a number of medications appear to be connected to symptoms of depression, including steroids, birth control pills, and the female hormone, estrogen. A relationship also may exist between certain types of beverages and depression, including sodas, chocolate, coffee and tea, which can lead to agitation when consumed and a depressive condition when withdrawn.

Hormonal Functioning in Women. Though the causes of

premenstrual syndrome and its relationship to depressive disorders are not clear, PMS is a problem for many women. Unfortunately, as women attempt to understand their mood swings by linking PMS with depression, they may create a self-defeating, self-fulfilling prophecy. That is, the belief that PMS is at the root of a woman's depression can consequently create the symptoms of depression associated with the menstrual cycle, thus fulfilling that expectation. Therefore, it is important to seek the expertise of a physician in order to ensure that the symptoms are not associated with the breakdown of some other bodily function or the result of a serious illness.

Researchers now suggest that the specific type of depression that health experts once believed menopausal women suffered from is no longer valid. It appears that women most vulnerable to menopausal depression typically are those with a history of past depressive episodes.[11]

A hormonal factor does appear to be implicated in the depression many women feel following childbirth, though the biological mechanism that would explain it has yet to be discovered. Postpartum depression can range from mild to seriously debilitating, and the symptoms can be exacerbated by the fatigue and stresses associated with parenting an infant. The help of a physician could rule out any other condition that the symptoms of depression may be masking.

Many women who are in their fifties and sixties today and lived their childhoods and early adult years during a time when Harriet Nelson and June Cleaver were their most impeccable role models have devoted their lives exclusively to the responsibilities of child rearing. When their children leave home, they often find themselves in the unenviable position of facing the empty nest, feeling that they have outlived their usefulness. The sense of loss that comes with the recognition that one can never regain that valued female function can catapult some women into a state of depression.

Psychosocial Factors. It is not clear whether psychosocial factors create a vulnerability to depression, affect the symptoms of the depressive episode, or occur as a result of the depression. Nevertheless, many of the same characteristics are shared by women who suffer from clinical depression. For example, the National Institute of Mental Health reported that in a study of a group of women with recurrent major depression, the subjects showed higher levels of interpersonal dependency needs than the norm, even when they were not depressed. The dependency was characterized by an increased need for recognition and approval and excess vulnerability to being hurt. However, more marked than their dependency needs was their social introversion. Both introversion (being withdrawn, shy, reserved, serious, and controlled) and neuroticism (the tendency to ruminate and be easily upset, moody or nervous) have been linked to certain types of depression.

Strong interpersonal dependency needs, low self-esteem, and feelings of helplessness often appear concurrently in clinically depressed women. Unfortunately, the factors are like a mobile responding to the breeze: No matter where the motion starts, the other parts will be affected. Hence, if a woman feels helpless about her ability to control her environment in an advantageous way, she will no doubt develop a low self-esteem, which likely will increase her need to be dependent on others. Furthermore, when a woman depends on others to do that which she perceives she is unable to do for herself, she prevents herself from developing a sense of control over her life, which, in turn, can reduce her level of self-esteem.

And closely linked to this dynamic is the observation that women who are being treated for depressive episodes often report that the stresses in their lives are overwhelming to them. As we saw in the case of Carolyn, the comment "I feel out-of-control" is a familiar one for many women. Some evidence suggests that there is a feminine vulnerability to becoming overwhelmed.

For example, a woman may become overwrought by a multitude of problems, feeling equally victimized by all of them and, therefore, feeling powerless over any of them. Accordingly, when we feel overwhelmed, we may temporarily lose our ability to prioritize, which leads to feeling even more overwhelmed. Men, on the other hand, tend to become more focused as they instinctively seek solutions to problems. Hence, the differences between the way in which men and women handle multiple stresses may create a depression risk factor for women.

At the present time, theories that link sex differences with the various classifications of depression are speculative and unproven. However, it appears that men still have an edge in the battle against depression—an edge that is probably attributable to the early socialization process. Traditionally, boys are taught to be assertive, self-reliant, product-oriented, logical, and decisive, while girls learn to be passive, dependent, cooperative, and process-oriented. As the differences in the socialization process narrow and girls learn to utilize skills traditionally taught boys, they may become less vulnerable to depression.

In the foregoing discussion, we have attempted to provide a brief overview of the multiple factors that exist and coexist with the occurrence of a clinical depression. Though the exact causes of depressive disorders are imprecise and not clearly understood, future research holds the key to the door of hope. Nevertheless, we are left with one important reassurance: Clinical depression is one of the most treatable of psychiatric problems.

THE TREATMENT OF DEPRESSION

While some depressed people do well with drug therapy, and some do well with psychotherapy, many do best with a combined treatment. Medication provides relatively quick relief of the acute symptoms of depression, and psychotherapy helps sufferers learn more effective ways of changing long-standing cognitive, emotional, or behavioral problems. Unfortunately, though a wide array of treatment options exist, it has been estimated that only 50 percent of the millions of people who suffer from clinical depression seek treatment of any kind. In the following discussion, we will explore some of the treatment methods available to those suffering from major depression. Unless otherwise specified, the information is based on the clinical experience of one of the authors, along with material published by the National Institute of Mental Health, which is available to the public.

Drug Therapy

When a person is diagnosed as clinically depressed according to the criteria in the Diagnostic and Statistical Manual of Mental Disorders, arrangements are generally made for referral to a medical doctor for an antidepressant evaluation. The physician might be a family doctor, although it is likely that the therapist will refer the person to a psychiatrist. Whether or not a depressed woman is placed on a regimen of medication for a trial period, she generally continues seeing her therapist to work on problems associated with the depression. If she is given an antidepressant, she must return to the medical doctor on a regular basis for monitoring of the drug dosage and to discuss any adverse effects the drug treatment might be causing. Since the response to drugs varies with each person, trials with several different drugs, or combinations of drugs, may be necessary to determine which is the most effective with fewest side effects.

MAO Inhibitors. The first breakthrough for the treatment of depression with drugs came about accidentally. In 1952, doctors who were treating tuberculosis patients discovered that the drug iproniazid had a remarkably euphoric effect on the emotional states of their patients. Toward the end of the 1950s, scientists learned why. Iproniazid falls into the category of anti-depressant medications known as MAO inhibitors, which block the breakdown of two neurotransmitters: norepinephrine and serotonin. The exact way in which these drugs work remains unknown, but they alter the action and distribution of brain chemicals. The MAO inhibitors appear to inhibit the action of a brain enzyme, monoamine oxidase (MAO), that destroys neuro-transmitters.

Patients who take MAO inhibitors must follow certain dietary and drug restrictions. For example, the interaction of these drugs with certain substances in some foods and beverages causes a quick and marked rise in blood pressure, which can increase the risk of hypertensive crisis and subsequent stroke. The condition is the result of an accumulation of tyramine, an amino acid that affects blood pressure. In addition, while most medications are quite compatible with MAO inhibitors, many interact adversely with this category of antidepressants, leading to hypertensive and other reactions.

MAO inhibitors are considered a second-line drug and are generally used when other categories of antidepressants either do not work or cannot be tolerated due to their side effects. However, they appear to be very useful for people who overeat and/or oversleep when depressed, as well as for those who also suffer from anxiety and phobias during their depression.

Tricyclic Antidepressants. A second category of antide-pressants, the tricyclics (named for their triple carbon chemical structure), increase the availability of neurotransmitters by slow-ing the rate at which they are reabsorbed by nerve cells. It is thought that these drugs prevent norepinephrine and serotonin neurotransmitters found within the synaptic gap from being re-turned to the sending neuron. Hence, by increasing their concen-tration within the tiny spaces between the nerve cells in the brain, more are made available for transmitting electrical impulses.

The side effects of tricyclics vary, but the most common are dry mouth, constipation, and urinary retention. As treatment proceeds, these side effects usually lessen or disappear.

Serotonin Reuptake Inhibitors. The third and newest category of medications preferentially and exclusively blocks the reabsorption of the neurotransmitter serotonin. Because of this specificity, medications such as Prozac, Paxil, Zoloft and Desyrel reverse the depressive symptoms with what is purported to be fewer of the bothersome side effects associated with other antidepressants.

Some people have alleged that Prozac can cause depressed people to engage in life-threatening behavior. However, it appears that the highly emotional discussions and news media reports of the past have quieted somewhat in view of current scientific data and medical opinion that support the view that Prozac does not cause suicide. According to the FDA's Psychopharmacological Drugs Advisory Committee, "There is no credible evidence of a causal link between the use of antidepressant drugs, including Prozac, and suicidality or violent behavior."[12]

Since the serotonin reuptake inhibitors were developed, questions have been raised about the way in which these drugs work. The world's leading antidepressant, Prozac, for example, has led some researchers to hypothesize that serotonin is the key regulator of mood, and that depression is essentially a shortfall of serotonin. Many questions about the serotonin reuptake inhibitors remain unanswered. As a *Time* magazine article asked: (a) Why do the tricyclics (which affect both norepinephrine and serotonin) work slightly better then the drugs like Prozac that work on the serotonin alone? (b) Why, since these drugs act quickly to change the serotonin levels in the brain, does it take up to a month for their effects to be felt?[13] As research continues, the answers to these and other questions about the connection between clinical depression and biochemical functions should be uncovered.

Electroconvulsive Therapy (ECT)

Like the drug therapies, electroconvulsive therapy (ECT) is a treatment procedure designed to reduce or eliminate the symptoms of psychological disorders by altering the way an individual's body functions. ECT, sometimes called "shock therapy," can be very helpful and even lifesaving for those few individuals who: (a) do not respond to drug therapy, (b) have concurrent medical problems that preclude use of medication, (c) are too depressed to engage effectively in psychotherapy, or (d) are at risk of suicide. ECT has been used for many decades, and today it is administered mainly to treat major depression.

The goal of ECT is to cause a seizure in the brain much like that which occurs spontaneously in some forms of epilepsy. A small electric current, lasting for one second or less, passes through two electrodes placed on an individual's head. The current excites neural tissue, stimulating a seizure that lasts for approximately one minute. Though it sounds as if the treatment would cause intolerable pain, the manner in which it is administered today involves little discomfort. ECT has been used effectively with many clinically depressed people; however, science is not certain why it works.

Psychotherapy

Whether or not drug therapy is prescribed for a depressed person, working with a professional therapist can be a significant aid to recovery. Psychotherapy is a formal process of interaction between an individual and a professional that helps the person recognize, define, and overcome personal and interpersonal difficulties. These problems could be in any of the following areas: cognitive (thought disorders), affective (emotional discomforts), and behaviorial (behavioral dysfunctions). Psychotherapy is not a useful treatment for people who are too disabled to talk rationally, or whose psychological state is so severe that they have lost contact with reality, as in the case of schizophrenia.

A few of the numerous systems of psychotherapy are specifically geared toward treating clinical depression. The most widely used systems include psychodynamic, supportive, cognitive, behavioral, and interpersonal therapies. The therapeutic process may include only the depressed individual, or it may include members of the family as well.

Though these various systems are considered distinct classifications of therapies, they contain many overlapping and interconnected characteristics. Hence, treatment might combine two systems of therapy, as it does in the cognitive/behaviorial approach.

Psychodynamic Therapy. Psychodynamic psychotherapy, the contemporary derivative of the psychoanalytic approach of Sigmund Freud, is one of the most widely used types of therapy. The approach seeks to treat the "whole person," rather than to simply provide "symptom relief." It views depression as a complex set of character problems stemming from the person's early childhood relationships with attachment figures such as parents or other close relatives. The approach involves bringing these early unresolved conflicts into the therapeutic setting where they can be dealt with and resolved. For women who tend to swallow their anger, depression is often described as anger turned inward. Therefore, psychodynamic therapists believe that uncovering, understanding, and dealing more effectively with these angry feelings may lead to recovery from depression.

The psychodynamic approach assumes that: (a) underlying processes, such as feelings, ideas, impulses, and drives, influence much of our observable behavior; (b) these underlying processes are often not at the conscious level; and (c) we frequently use defense mechanisms to keep anxiety-provoking feelings, ideas, and impulses out of conscious awareness. One of the mechanisms that helps people explore conflict is the psychological phenomenon called "transference." Transference is the therapeutic process in which the individual in treatment "transfers" perceptions and feelings about important childhood figures (usually a parent) onto the therapist. Hence, the individual responds to the therapist as though he or she were a significant figure from the past. For example, a woman in therapy may be helped to recognize that she is perceiving an authoritarian, critical mother in the person of the therapist. The therapist can then help her explore ways this vulnerability to authority and criticism are interfering with her "here and now" relationships so she can change any maladaptive behavior that may be a carry-over from the past.

Another dynamic that surfaces in psychodynamic therapy is the condition called "regression." It is a defense mechanism that occurs when an individual responds to anxiety by behaving in a way that characterizes a previous developmental stage. Regression means "moving backward"; in psychodynamic therapy, it means returning to an earlier and generally less mature behavior.

In therapeutic settings, it is not uncommon for stress to evoke the regression mechanism. When stress becomes too great, a person may begin sobbing like a child, or may try to reduce anxiety by running out of the therapy session. These behaviors are unconscious efforts to protect the fragile ego and reduce the state of anxiety. And, though these earlier habits led to satisfaction in the past, they work only temporarily to reduce stress. Unfortunately, if our behavior is dominated by these defenses, we are prevented from facing the demands of reality, as well as the conditions that created the onset of the stress.

As psychodynamic therapists attempt to help a person develop more realistic appraisals of relationships and identify and seek out healthy relationships with others, they are generally very active in the therapeutic process. Therefore, they are likely to question, confront, and offer interpretations about the maladaptive ways the client is behaving.

Supportive Therapy. Many women tend to feel they are losing control as they attempt to cope with multiple stressors in their lives. Many also appear to shoulder the blame when attempts to cope with their stressors seem to fail. Supportive psychotherapy seeks to bolster a depressed person's self-esteem, to assist that person in developing an understanding of what constitutes realistic and unrealistic expectations, and to encourage clients to feel more hopeful.

Often, depressed women enter therapy believing they cannot be helped. Even worse, some believe they don't deserve to be helped. It is as though they have been relegated to a life of hopeless despair. Women who are able to resolve the issues underlying their depression do so by changing this perception of victimization. In addition, they seem to achieve a more realistic understanding of what therapy can and cannot do. That is, they recognize that the success of therapy is not just another stroke of luck, nor the result of magical answers emanating from a therapist. Rather, successful therapeutic outcomes result from an internal will to engage in self-determined treatment. The therapist's genuine belief in an individual's resilience, as well as a sense of optimism about the person's ability to succeed, can provide the contagion of hopefulness that individuals need as they garner the courage to confront their conflicts.

In an accepting climate of empathy and caring, the therapist helps a client to become more self-accepting. In turn, through a bolstered self-esteem, a woman is more likely to move away from the erroneous perception that control of her life is dependent upon external factors. And, as this movement takes place, so does the transition from her perception that the therapist is an authority figure with all the answers to the recognition that the woman herself has the ability to make decisions and move from a state of helplessness and hopelessness to a state of self-control and inner-directed confidence.

Cognitive Therapy. Whether negative self-talk is the cause of depression or the result of the illness is not clear. However, what is known is that depressed people have a tendency toward self-damaging, irrational thought processes. The cognitive model of depression suggests that depressed persons believe that enormous demands exist and that immense barriers block access to goals. They believe that current troubles will not improve and that they lack the ability to cope or control an event's outcome. Hence, they are reluctant to even commit themselves to a goal; and the indecisiveness that is so commonplace among depressed people reflects their belief that they are incapable of making correct decisions. The goal of cognitive therapy is to correct negative thinking habits and, as a result, lift depressed feelings. Cognitive therapists believe that the way to change feelings, and maladaptive behaviors associated with those feelings, is to change negative thought patterns.

One of the widely used approaches aimed at dispelling the myths underlying negative self-talk is Rational-Emotive Therapy, which views cognition, emotion, and behavior as integrated. The basic premise is that people's emotions and behaviors are determined by how the individual views the world and cognitively interprets beliefs, evaluations, and reactions to life experiences. The approach handles profound depression by showing sufferers quickly, directly, and vigorously that they are probably causing their depression by: (a) blaming themselves for what they have done or not done, (b) castigating themselves for being depressed and inert, and (c) bemoaning their fate because of the hassles and harshness of environmental conditions.[14]

This therapeutic approach teaches individuals the skills that help them identify and dispute irrational beliefs (e.g., "Everyone must like me") that have been acquired and are now maintained by self-indoctrination. It is an educational process that teaches the learner strategies for "straight thinking" that can be practiced in real life. And, when therapy is ended, individuals are able to take the skill of rational thinking with them to observe, understand, and continue to persistently attack their irrational, self-defeating thought patterns.

Behavioral Therapy. Behavioral therapists attempt to alleviate depression by helping people change maladaptive behaviors that result from depression. The therapies focus on the individual's current problems and the factors influencing them, as opposed to past events. Hence, to behaviorists, understanding the origin of a psychological problem is not essential for producing a change in behavior.

Because behavioral therapies assume that depressive behaviors are learned and reinforced in the environment, the major goals of therapy are to change not only the individual's behavior, but also the associated interactions with the environment that are unpleasant for the individual. Therefore, throughout the action-oriented course of therapy, the individual assesses problem behaviors and the conditions that are maintaining them. Treatment goals are established in concrete and objective terms in order to be able to specify and measure results. And strategies are tailor-made to meet the unique needs of the individual.

Though this list is not exhaustive, some of the strategies that might be learned during the treatment session and implemented during and between the sessions are: relaxation, assertiveness and social skills training; and self-control procedures, logging, self-monitoring, role-playing, and systematic desensitization.

As an example, the self-monitoring strategy could be used by a woman like Carolyn, who, you may recall, complained about standing alone in her kitchen eating junk food. Carolyn could begin the self-monitoring process by determining how often she does this each week, and then setting manageable goals for reducing or eventually eliminating this type of behavior. For example, she could decide to spend a half hour eating dinner at the kitchen table two evenings the first week, three evenings the second week, and so on. She could record these goals for changing her eating habits on a chart and then check off her successful attempts. She might develop a reward system for herself to increase the likelihood of achieving her goals.

With this technique, Carolyn will soon recognize that she is not helpless, but rather has the capacity to change her behavior. While achieving this limited goal will not necessarily end Carolyn's loneliness and depression, it is one step toward helping her eliminate an unpleasant habit associated with her depression.

Interpersonal Therapy. This approach is based on the concept that depression occurs within the context of disturbed personal and social relationships. When relationships fail, as in the case of divorce, individuals may be vulnerable to depression. In other cases, depression can create the catalyst for a disruption in relationships. In either case, the depressed person treated by an interpersonal therapist learns both the nature of clinical depression and the connection between that depression and the relationship situation.

A "here and now" approach to therapy is used to help the depressed person confront feelings that are associated with relationships and to resolve interpersonal problems. In addition, the therapist helps the depressed woman develop social and behavioral strategies that will maximize her potential for developing more fulfilling personal relationships. One of the major tenets of this approach is that as social functioning improves, so will the symptoms of depression.

Groups Versus Individual Therapy. Though the systems of therapy discussed above are commonly associated with individual counseling, group counseling also utilizes successfully some of the same therapeutic approaches. For example, behavioral, cognitive, or interpersonal therapy can be used quite effectively within the group setting for the treatment of a variety of depressions.

Participation in groups should be used guardedly as a treatment for individuals who may be so withdrawn, fragile, suspicious, or hostile that social interaction can cause additional stress for themselves and the group membership. For some depressed women, however, groups may have a distinct advantage over the more traditional, individual psychotherapeutic strategies. For example, participants in groups are able to: (a) explore their style of relating to others in groups and to learn more effective social skills, (b) gain support for new behaviors that they may want to use in the "real world," (c) recreate the everyday world within the group, since many groups are comprised of diverse memberships with respect to age, interest, background, etc., (d) learn from the membership about themselves and experience emotional closeness and caring with others who identify with their conflicts, and (e) identify empathically with the struggles of other group members.

However, unless the intervention is on an inpatient basis, outpatient groups do not always afford the consistency and continuity that individual therapy can provide. The dropout rate can be high in some outpatient groups, and new members often are permitted to enter a group after the original membership has been formed. In addition, it often is far more difficult to maintain confidentiality in group settings. Finally, some individuals who have participated in groups often complain that group members frequently seem only to want to vent their pain and don't seem to be motivated to move toward positive behavioral change.

The credentials of the group facilitator should be examined by anyone considering group counseling. Is the group facilitator a certified or licensed therapist, or is it someone who has started a splinter group from one in which he or she has previously been a participant? The group process can create a certain degree of crisis and turmoil even under optimal conditions; an incompetent leader who lacks skills in handling the process can cause undue, and sometimes excessive, psychological damage to participants. In addition, in the absence of experienced leadership, it takes only one hostile, deviant, or narcissistically self-serving group member to sabotage group interaction and cohesion and destroy a climate of safety and acceptance. Under these conditions, the potential for members to achieve their personal goals may be severely hampered.

For some depressed individuals, it can be quite advantageous to participate in both individual and group counseling. In individual therapy a client is able to determine both the conscious and unconscious root causes of her depression and learn new ways of thinking and behaving. At the same time, particularly for depressed women who have experienced loss through separation and divorce, the group setting can provide opportunities to develop meaningful connections within a supportive network of people. Before learning is transferred to the real world, groups can also provide a safe setting for rehearsing the learning that has taken place in individual therapy.

Few adults can foresee what lies ahead when they consider divorce. For some, divorce can be a healthy catalyst for social, psychological, and economic change and a renewed sense of stability. For others, however, it can be an agent of change that will usher in a tidal wave of intense anger, loneliness, sadness, fear, anxiety, and grief. These highly charged emotional states can interact to become the precursors to one of our nation's major health hazards: clinical depression. And, when left untreated, clinical depression can produce a force that is so strong that an individual's defenses against self-destructive impulses collapse.

We have attempted in this chapter to increase awareness of the symptoms and probable causes of the illness, and, by doing so, serve as a prevention mechanism for women who may be contemplating or going through the process of divorce. For those who currently suffer from the characteristic symptoms of the illness, the information is intended to encourage appropriate treatment. At this moment, ten to fourteen million people in the United States have a diagnosable depression. And it has been estimated that over the course of a lifetime, approximately 25 percent of the population will experience a major depressive episode. Further, it has been suggested that after a first episode, about 70 percent can expect to face major depression again, with the median number of four recurrences during a lifetime.[15] In addition, when we factor into the equation alcoholism and drug abuse that are caused by or related to depression, the economic costs are staggering: the estimated annual price tag for treatment, job absenteeism, lowered productivity, and permanent withdrawal from the work force because of illness or death is well over $100 billion! But far greater than the dollar amounts are the human costs to the social and emotional quality of the lives of those who suffer from depression and its consequences.

CHECKLIST

The following checklist has been devised as a guide for diagnosing one kind of depression, major depression, a common diagnosis for depression requiring treatment. The statements have been adapted from the 1994 criteria developed by the American Psychiatric Association.[16]

Directions: Respond to each of the following statements with a true or false. Read each statement carefully and consider whether the symptom: (1) has been present continuously for a two-week period or more and (2) represents a change from previous ways you have functioned.

T   F

☐ ☐ 1. I have noticed a marked change in my appetite nearly every day and have experienced a significant weight gain or weight loss that is not attributable to dieting.

☐ ☐ 2. I have noticed a marked change in my sleeping patterns nearly every day (i. e., either sleeping too much or inability to sleep).

☐ ☐ 3. I have lost interest or pleasure in all, or almost all, activities most of the day, nearly every day.

☐ ☐ 4. I feel fatigued and experience a loss of energy nearly every day.

☐ ☐ 5. Nearly every day, I experience feelings of excessive or inappropriate guilt or feelings of worthlessness.

T F

☐ ☐ 6. Nearly every day I find myself having difficulty concentrating or thinking, or experience indecisiveness.

☐ ☐ 7. I feel restless or slowed down nearly every day and it is observable by others.

☐ ☐ 8. I have recurring thoughts of death or thoughts of suicide (with or without a plan).

☐ ☐ 9. I experience a persistent depressed mood most of the day, nearly every day.

Note: Adapted and reprinted with permission, from the *Diagnostic and Statistical Manual of Mental Disorders*, Fourth Edition, Copyright 1994 American Psychiatric Association.

Evaluating your level of depression. According to the American Psychiatric Association's criteria, you may be suffering from major depression if:

1. You have had at least five of the symptoms continually for a two-week period or more and these symptoms represent a change from previous functioning, and,

2. At least one of the symptoms is either number 3 (diminished interest or pleasure) or number 9 (depressed mood).

Remember, a diagnosis of depression rests on numerous factors which, when weighed together, can determine whether an individual is suffering from major depression and could benefit from treatment. Therefore, if you meet the above criteria, you should consider seeking the advice of your physician in order to determine whether your symptoms are serious enough to require a medical and/or psychological intervention.

5

THE GRIEVING PROCESS

Patricia, 55, reflected upon her divorce and the range of emotions she felt over the loss:

"Making the decision to get a divorce took me nearly ten years. I was one of those women who was looking for the 'right' time to end the relationship. I wanted to wait until my children were older so they'd be better prepared to survive the divorce.

"But I now realize that there's seldom a 'right' time to divorce, as far as the children are concerned. They can lose either way. In my own case, by making the choice to stay in the relationship for ten years, my children lived for a decade in an unhealthy atmosphere—a climate that was short on stability and long on deception. On the other hand, if I had chosen to leave ten years earlier, my children would have felt the pain of loss at a very young age. As it turns out, I simply postponed their grieving until a later date.

"But I certainly didn't delay my pain as I struggled with my unspoken decision. I had so many intense feelings. And often, just as I thought I had healed from the pain of one emotion, another would take its place. I felt like I was on an emotional roller coaster going nowhere.

"And I'd frequently vacillate from one feeling to another. Sometimes I felt rage when I thought of the role my husband had played in the breakdown of our marriage. At other times I would deny that things were really as bad as I thought. There were times when I would remember what I wanted to forget, and times when I would forget what I wanted to remember.

"But it seemed ironic that going through all that grief and pain for so long before my divorce didn't make me immune to such feelings when my marriage finally ended. New issues surfaced after my divorce, and as I struggled with them, old pains returned along with new emotions. I had an enormous sense of guilt for having changed history. Things would never be the same for me, for my children, or for the family we once knew.

"But I learned to confront those emotional lows and try to use the pain to find self-understanding and recovery. I now realize that whether loss is anticipated, as it was for me for 10 years, or real, as it was on the day of my divorce, the pain of loss is normal and expected. It's nature's way of letting us know that something needs to be healed.

"For me, just as it is for so many other women who have grieved the loss of a significant relationship, the process of grieving was a very private experience of healing from within. Unlike happiness, which is an emotional contagion eager to be shared with others, grief is a deeply personal experience encountered in the silence of one's own heart."

As Patricia discovered, grief is a predictable and necessary personal response to loss. It is the mass of human emotion that is experienced when there is a major change in our lives from what has been familiar and significant to us. Anticipatory grief is the term applied to grief expressed in advance of a loss when the loss is perceived as inevitable. Acute grief is the intense grief that follows a loss. A person's reactions to the stages of anticipatory and acute grief are similar.

Loss precipitates powerful feelings, and those of us who are able to summon the courage to face our moment-to-moment emotions, as painful as they may be, can begin to acknowledge "this too is me" and move toward self-healing and recovery.

However, if we are unable or unwilling to work through our grief, healing can be a lengthy and painful journey. The Zeigarnik Effect, a well-known principle in psychology, might explain why the process of letting go of a loss is so difficult for people who are unable to look grief in the face. Essentially, the phenomenon refers to the universal tendency to remember more about unfinished tasks rather than tasks that have been completed. Until accomplished, unfinished tasks can produce tension, which, in turn, can become a major source of irritation and a silent reminder that there is work to be done. Similarly, if we deny the existence of our intense emotions and try to avoid the critical task of grief work, we are unable to recover from the painful loss from which we are trying to escape. We are left with ongoing tension emanating from unfinished business.

While some people try to avoid the normal emotional response to grief, others who want to face their pain may not know how to do so effectively. They often do not understand the variety of ways unresolved grief can manifest itself. For example, a woman undergoing therapy for clinical depression following a stressful divorce might say she wants to find a way to "get rid" of the terrible dreams she is having about her ex-husband. The therapist may tell her that persons who are depressed during a stressful time in their lives appear to work through their depression more successfully when they dream with strong feelings and incorporate the stressor directly into their dreams.[1] Then the woman is likely to see her dreams as helpful and to change her mind about wanting to get rid of them. Over time, as her dreams are examined, she has the potential for resolving her conflict, reducing her depressive symptoms, and healing from her loss.

Grief is an active, not a passive, process that must be accomplished over time in order for one to recover from loss. However, it is a mistake to think that time alone heals the pain of grief. We are reminded of Janet, in a previous chapter, who, when looking back at her own process of recovery, ruminated whether "it is really time itself that dulls the pain of the past, or what we do with our time that makes the difference." Like Janet, those who have gone through the grieving process learn that it is not time alone that heals, but the way in which time is used that determines how long the pain remains acute, whether it is ever fully experienced, and how long the process of recovery will take.

Henry David Thoreau eloquently expressed the consequence of time ill-spent in his words, "As though we could kill time, without injuring eternity." Women who choose to "kill" time in the aftermath of the loss of a relationship through divorce jeopardize their recovery: They are unable to maximize their potential for discovering opportunities for personal growth and change. Hence, whether we choose to remain single or eventually decide to remarry, what we discover about ourselves as we make wise use of our time during the process of recovery can have a significant impact on our future well-being. (The final section of this chapter provides some helpful hints about ways in which time can be used effectively during the grieving process.)

When we think of grief as a process, we are indebted to the important contribution of Dr. Elisabeth Kubler-Ross, who helped clarify the stages of grief in her book *On Death and Dying*.[2] Dr. Kubler-Ross depicted five stages: (1) denial, (2) anger, (3) bargaining, (4) depression, (5) acceptance.

Though these stages were defined by Dr. Kubler-Ross to describe the path toward acceptance for a dying patient, most of these stages are also present when we experience anticipatory or acute grief associated with the loss of a love relationship.

The grief model that is identified in this chapter includes a number of stages that resemble those found in Dr. Kubler-Ross's work. Our model, however, includes additional emotional steps to recovery that have been experienced by women who have suffered the pain of loss through divorce. It is important to understand, however, that for each woman, grieving is an intensely personal journey toward recovery. And while we will describe the stages as distinct and sequential categories, people generally do not move through them in an orderly fashion. Some people start at one stage, while others begin at another. Some individuals experience all of the stages, while others experience a few. There are those who may experience one stage and return to it at a later date. And some may experience a particular stage only fleetingly, while others remain in that stage for a very long time—weeks or even months.

Moreover, the direction the grieving process takes, its duration, and the intensity of the associated pain also depend on a variety of situational factors. These include the length of the marriage, the underlying causes of the breakup, whether children are involved, the age of the partners, whether or not other crises are occurring at the time of the divorce, and the financial status of the partners at the time of the marital rupture. Hence, the road traveled during the grieving process is unique to each individual and cannot be precisely predicted.

THE GRIEVING PROCESS: TEN STAGES TOWARD RECOVERY

The following grief model consists of ten emotional stages toward recovery: (1) Denial, (2) Bargaining, (3) Guilt and Shame, (4) Fear, (5) Regret, (6) Depression, (7) Anger, (8) Aloneness, (9) Acceptance and (10) Freedom. Regardless of the unique experience that loss through divorce produces, and irrespective of whether the woman is leaving her husband or being left by him, she should be prepared to face some or all of these steps in her climb toward personal growth and freedom.

Stage One: Denial

During the stage of denial, individuals frequently describe themselves as experiencing numbness or shock when the decision to divorce is announced. This state of numbness, which is intricately tied to one's sense of disbelief, is not only experienced by the spouse who is left behind. A young woman who had decided to file for divorce after six years of marriage described her emotional state in this way: "I feel stunned and disconnected from my feelings. It feels like my body is in one place, my mind is in another, and my feelings are somewhere else. Nothing is in sync. I feel like this can't really be happening. I don't know what I'm going to do with the rest of my life. . . .

"It's not like I haven't thought about this for a long time. I have put up with a lot because I've wanted to be sure that I was doing the right thing. But even though this is my idea, I don't want this to happen. I know it has to happen, though. I can't back out now; everyone knows."

During denial, a dreamlike state surfaces, sometimes described as a "mental and emotional paralysis," which can interfere with one's perception of reality. It is not unusual, for example, to see a woman who is being left trying to "win back" the departing partner and behaving as though nothing is really going to happen. A woman who engages in maneuvers of self-deception that trick her into believing that a partner is not going to leave prevents herself from experiencing other normal and expected emotional responses to loss.

In addition, denial is a powerful mechanism that prevents partners from recognizing the role they have played in the disintegration of the marriage. And to no one's surprise, as people engage in behaviors that deny problems, they may perpetuate the problem even further by behaving in ways that created the division between the partners in the first place. For example, a man might become even more of an isolate than he was before the announcement, thinking that his wife needs space to "get herself together," not recognizing that she has been intensely lonely throughout their marriage. Or a woman might become even more possessive, thinking she needs to provide more emotional closeness, not realizing that her husband has felt suffocated for many years.

When the stage of denial lifts and partners reconcile themselves to the fact that divorce is inevitable, the next stage in the grieving process emerges.

Stage Two: Bargaining

During this stage of the grieving process, the person being left often tries to "cut a deal." John, in Chapter Three, referred to his attempts at bargaining with his comment: "When she told me six months ago that we were through, I tried so hard to change. I really believed we could work things out." Like so many others who discover a spouse's intention to divorce, John agreed to do whatever he had to do to get his wife to change her mind. Unfortunately, people who are willing to do anything to get a partner to reconsider can become suggestible, vulnerable, and easily manipulated by spouses with limited integrity. And one's own needs, identity, and sense of self-worth can be lost when trying to cajole or "please" the other person into staying in the marriage.

During the divorce process, the illusion of keeping togetherness alive, which is inherent in the bargaining stage, manifests itself in potentially serious ways. For example, because it is not unusual to feel lonely during this stage of the grieving process, couples who are splitting up may find themselves slipping into sexual encounters. Having sex with a partner who is saying goodbye is not the same as healthy intimacy. Sexual activity under these conditions keeps alive only an illusion of intimacy between partners. The only purpose it does serve is to help the needy feel needed and to help the guilty feel redeemed.

Similarly, celebrating the holidays together, going to church together, or traveling together to watch a child compete in a sports event may offer an analgesic that reduces some of the pain of loss. However, such actions send mixed signals to the partner who is being left, as well as to the couple's children.

Divorce means saying goodbye, and the bargaining stage often prevents people from doing just that. The obvious danger is that when people don't say goodbye, they may get back together for the wrong reasons—to avoid the loneliness and unhappiness associated with ending the love relationship.

Stage Three: Guilt and Shame

The painful emotions of guilt and shame found in stage three frequently overlap with the experiences of the previous stage when people attempt to bargain for the return of their partners. Though the terms guilt and shame are often used interchangeably in our society, there are several important distinctions between the two concepts.

Guilt, which is generally measured by society's expectations, is the emotional response to wrongdoing; it is associated with the belief that we should atone for having hurt someone for whom we care. In the case of divorce, guilt is frequently experienced first by the person ending the relationship. On the other hand, shame, which is synonymous with humiliation and the opposite of self-esteem, can occur any time we fail to live up to our own self-imposed expectations. During divorce, shame is likely to be experienced by the person who is left, who may feel responsible for the failed marriage.

A further distinction between the two concepts can be seen in the way those who experience guilt or shame seek relief from their symptoms. When we feel guilty, we welcome forgiveness and confession; therefore when we speak of the source of our guilt, the associated pain is diminished. Shame, on the other hand, invites neither forgiveness nor confession, because we recoil from facing our shame and the feelings of failure and inferiority that have produced it. Those who experience the painful effect of shame fear being discovered; therefore, their shame induces hiding and concealment. Consequently, because the source, experience, and feelings associated with shame remain unspoken, sufferers are unable to find appropriate emotional release. Instead, those who experience shame develop elaborate defenses such as anger, envy, contempt, and/or depression to protect any discovery of the flawed, shame soaked self.

As partners face the reality that their marriage is going to end, the two often inseparable emotions of guilt and shame inevitably emerge. For example, if a man leaves his wife, guilt is reflected in thoughts like "How can I do this to her?" or "How can I do this to my children?" In turn, his wife might respond to his decision to leave by thinking, "What have I done to make him want to leave?" reflecting the shame she is experiencing for believing she has failed.

In our society, women often blame themselves for failures even when they clearly are not responsible for the mistakes; consequently, a woman may experience shame whether she leaves the relationship or she is left. In addition, if a woman initiates the divorce, she compounds her emotional vulnerability by experiencing both guilt and shame as she laments, "How can I do this to my family?" (guilt), and "What have I done to create this terrible situation?" (shame). The intensity of these two painful emotions may provide sufficient cause for her to rethink, and perhaps even reverse, her decision to leave the relationship.

Guilt and shame pervade the lives of almost all couples who suffer loss through divorce. And the two emotional dynamics can work together to exacerbate the problems that already exist when relationships end. For example, because guilt often renders a person vulnerable to the manipulations of a partner experiencing shame, unhealthy concessions to pacify the "victim" often are made, such as returning to the family home and living in a spare room, or returning for brief sexual liaisons. As in the previous stage of bargaining, the willingness to engage in these behaviors can be misleading and dangerous. Hence, while a brief return to the family home may reduce one's guilt for leaving in the first place, and may momentarily appear to enhance the other partner's self-esteem, each partner reunites with the other with a very different set of motives, desires, and expectations.

Euphoria, under these conditions, is only temporary. And the good feelings soon give way to attacks of shame and guilt. For example, a woman may experience increased shame, feeling she has not only failed in her marriage but also is developing a growing dependence upon her spouse in order to feel less empty. And her husband, who already feels guilty for having rejected his spouse, now feels even more guilt for creating an illusion of intimacy when, in reality, he knows that the mutual bond of love no longer exists.

Recognizing that guilt and shame are a normal part of the grieving process is essential to healing. To reduce one's painful feelings of guilt and to move beyond this stage, the person needs to recognize and communicate the source and the feelings of guilt being experienced. In addition, it is important for those experiencing guilt to understand that when the decision to leave a relationship was not made to abuse power or to cause intentional harm to a spouse, it is inappropriate to harbor feelings of guilt. It is far healthier to consider the possibility that the choice was guided by the decision-maker's sense of integrity, genuine caring for the other person, and/or the desire to promote the possibility of future happiness and hope for both partners.

To handle painful feelings of shame effectively requires that individuals lower their "expectation thermostats" to achieve a more realistic level of internal demands. It also requires a clearer understanding of the elements that constitute a healthy relationship so that we aren't tempted to own all the "fault" for what went wrong. If we are able to talk openly about our shame with a skilled professional, we can significantly reduce the painful feelings and avoid developing unhealthy defense mechanisms to disguise them. Our feelings of shame likely will recede when the damaged self-esteem is repaired through self-understanding, and the wounds are replaced by a healthy sense of self-respect. Painful as it is, shame can be healed for those who have the courage to confront this and every other stage in their unique process of grieving.

Stage Four: Fear

When a woman experiences loss through divorce, unrealistic fear is a common outcome. This is particularly true of the woman who has never spent a prolonged period of time living independently prior to her marriage or who has not developed a healthy sense of independence in the home prior to the breakup.

Unlike realistic fear, which surfaces when our anxieties are derived from real dangers that exist in the external world, unrealistic or neurotic fear is rooted in threats that seem to have no rational basis. When a woman is asked about such fear, which often borders on terror, it frequently doesn't even make sense to her. The woman knows intellectually there is no real basis for the fear she is experiencing, and she may say, "I know it doesn't make sense to worry about these things. I've never worried about them before. And I know that I can handle them; I'm just afraid to think I will have to."

"These things" that the woman refers to are often related to the tasks and situations she will now be responsible for as a single person. The tasks, which often were assumed by the partner before the divorce, suddenly take on a kind of mystique, suggesting to a woman that she is not equipped to handle the problems herself. At this point, she probably is not even aware of those tasks she can accomplish, or whom to call for help for those she cannot.

It is within this context that the cyclone of neurotic fear begins to gain momentum. She anticipates the possibility of having to deal with things that during the marriage generated no anxiety: she worries about fixing leaky faucets, and unplugging clogged drains, and turning off the water supply in the house, and repairing shingles on the roof that could be blown away by the wind, and bleeding the furnace, and fixing the garbage disposal, and getting mice out of the garage, and paying her bills on time. In addition, she worries about being alone, being stalked, being raped in the parking lot of the mall, receiving prank calls, sleeping too little, or sleeping too much. She worries about herself, and she worries about her children. And sometimes she even worries about worrying.

It is true that women in our society are particularly vulnerable to potentially threatening situations (for example, walking to one's car in the dark), and they need to develop a vigilant, healthy caution to avoid trouble. But many of the fears they dread are not life-threatening. To the casual observer they may even appear absurd. For example, one of the major anxieties a woman may develop, particularly if she has had to return to the job market, is that her car will break down. She places great importance upon her car and often fears that it will stop running, or blow a tire, or begin to leak oil. To a man this fear may seem preposterous; to a woman the fear, though irrational, creates anxiety beyond reason. But it isn't the car problems themselves that create a woman's fears; it is, rather, the fact that her livelihood may be threatened if her means of transportation is obstructed. She also fears being helplessly isolated and stranded in a threatening situation if her car breaks down at night. And, if she has children who depend on her for transportation to school, lessons, sports and other activities, the thought of an inoperable car conjures up more anxieties.

As unrealistic fears are compounded, they can immobilize a woman to the point that she may, in fact, be unable to handle everyday problems. And if she doesn't seek professional help, either through medication by a physician or psychotherapy, her anxieties can lead to a full-blown panic attack. This can lead to sleeping problems, dizziness, palpitations, accelerated heart rate, hyperventilation, uncontrollable sweating, or racing thoughts. At its worse, a woman may begin to feel so vulnerable and helpless, and become so fearful of what appears to her to be a hostile and frightening world, that she may develop a classic case of agoraphobia, not wanting to leave the safety of her home at all. Those who suffer from panic can be reminded that panic does not attack, but they can attack panic! And, the earlier the symptoms of panic are dealt with, the sooner they can be controlled.

While some women get medical attention for their fears, many do not seek adequate help. Unfortunately, as a woman becomes more and more overwhelmed by her fears, it is likely that her obsessive worrying, self-perceptions of incompetence, and inability to focus on handling the tasks at hand will result in feelings of disgust toward herself. She may feel lonely and long for her ex-partner, who she now believes is capable of eliminating the fear she is experiencing. Even if the woman has initiated the divorce, the reasons for bailing out can be dimmed by the many unrealistic fears that present themselves during this stage. And too often it is these underlying, irrational fears that are at the root of obsessive thoughts of regret about the marital rupture and fantasies about an idealized ex-partner.

Stage Five: Regret

The emotions of extreme fear and loneliness that emerge during the previous stage can become the impetus for feelings of regret. Healthy regret—which is heard in the final stages of the grieving process when people have accepted their loss—is reflected in thoughts such as, "It is very sad that the relationship had to end, but I am now able to go on with the rest of my life, and I hope my ex-partner will be able to do the same." However, regret at this stage of the grieving process sounds more like

"What have I done? When I look back, he really wasn't such a bad guy. There is no way that I am going to be able to handle all this on my own. I should never have allowed this to happen!"

Barry Lubetkin and Elena Oumano point out in their book *Bailing Out: The Healthy Way to Get Out of a Bad Relationship and Survive*[3] that because a person often is very uncomfortable with the choice that is made, the alternative that was not chosen frequently takes on a greater value in one's mind and contributes to feelings of regret during "postdecision rumination." It is in this way that a person begins to idealize a partner and to question one's own motives for having left the relationship. The resulting ambivalence creates a state of aversion and tension, which we then seek to reduce or avoid.

In an attempt to relieve this tension, the woman may look to others to help justify her decision and to gain support and reassurance that the choice was the appropriate one. In addition, altering distorted thought patterns and replacing them with more rational, adaptive ones can also help reduce her ambivalence. For example, she might replace the thought "I should not have left my husband; he was the only one who knew how to control the kids" with "In the past I was not expected to discipline the children, but that doesn't mean I can't learn the skills of effective parenting."

As people attempt to deal with their ambivalence and their simultaneous feelings of attraction toward and repulsion from the source of their tension, they often move from idealizing to devaluing their partners. They get hooked by resentment, which may feel good at first but only serves to keep old wounds open and festering for a long time. It traps us and prevents us from taking steps toward recovery. By giving up resentment, we free ourselves to accept the reality that a marriage that was once alive is now dead. By doing this, we can then be challenged to create a new and healthier life for ourselves.

Another emotion that surfaces briefly during this stage of

the grieving process is anger. Anger at this point is tentative because the separation continues to be perceived, by one or both partners, as reversible. As one divorced woman recently confided, "It was a mini-anger that returned later after a long period of terrible sadness." Perhaps another reason why the anger at this stage is brief and less intense is that women in our society are "intropunitive"—they tend to punish themselves for their own anger rather than expressing it outwardly. And anger turned inward becomes one of the major causes of depression.

Stage Six: Depression

Regardless of whether this stage occurs during the separation process or long after the divorce, it is critical that people confront and not swallow feelings of depression that inevitably surface when relationships end.

Depression can take many forms, ranging from a low-grade feeling of despondency that comes with sadness and disappointment, to an intense and often incapacitating episode of clinical depression. The previous chapter has provided an in-depth look at the more severe state of major depression. Therefore, we will focus here on the less debilitating state of depression that typically emerges during this stage of the grieving process.

A woman who suffers loss through divorce commonly complains of many of the same uncomfortable feelings that one suffers during a major depression. However, the symptoms do not have the same intensity and duration. She may complain of insomnia, excessive crying, fatigue, anxiety, restlessness, guilt, or difficulty concentrating and/or making decisions. However, she usually bounces back and, within a reasonable length of time, begins to accept the reality of her loss and resigns herself to the fact that the marriage is over.

Signs of resignation and acceptance were recently shared by a woman who was approaching the end of this stage of the grieving process: "I feel so sad that our marriage didn't work out. I feel as though a part of me died when my husband left. I still feel empty, and I know I will feel this way for a long, long time. We knew each other since college, and we had our own personal history together. When I think of my husband spending his life with someone else, I get a stabbing pain in the pit of my stomach. If I think of my husband ever having sex with another person, I feel like vomiting. I know we didn't get along, but it's painful when I think he will share himself, his dreams, his hopes with another person someday. I guess I'll have to do that, too, and the dreams and hopes will probably take new forms. Life is going to be different."

Though the woman had not yet come to terms with her anger, she was trying to confront the reality that though her relationship was over, it didn't mean her life was over.

The extent to which a woman is able to cope with the change that has occurred in her life is frequently put to the test on the day her ex-husband is re-married. There is considerable evidence that a man is more likely to re-marry sooner than his ex-wife; furthermore, many divorced women are choosing not to re-marry. Therefore, the ex-wife may have to face his wedding day as a single person. This can be a very difficult time, but careful planning will help the woman cope. For example, planning a party or being with close friends can help her avoid a downward spiral of sadness that can prolong her stay in Stage Six.

Divorced women may face the temptation to lift the pain of sadness and loneliness by prematurely forming a new, intimate bond with the opposite sex. When a close relationship is begun before the grieving process has reached completion, it generally will not withstand the test of time. It is not unusual for lonely divorced people to be drawn together. But one or both of them may come to the encounter with a truckload of soiled laundry. The laundry baskets are branded with the trademark "TROUBLE" if one or both of the individuals has suffered a marital breakup and the grief has not been resolved. Sometimes we reveal our laundry before it is prudent to do so, and the other person escapes through the nearest exit. Sometimes we wait so long that when it finally is placed in full view, the other person feels betrayed because no invitation was extended at an earlier time to see it. And sometimes we never show the other person what is in our baskets; we use the new relationship to work through all the unresolved emotions that are left in them, including feelings of guilt, shame, fear, regret, resentment, distrust, anger, and sadness. And if this relationship ends, we fill up our baskets with more soiled laundry and move on.

It can be both healthy and helpful to develop friendships with both the same and opposite sex during the grieving process. Healthy, platonic relationships can significantly reduce feelings of loneliness and detachment during a difficult transitional period. But the above metaphor suggests that one should be very cautious about becoming involved in an intimate relationship while there is grief work to be done.

Stage Seven: Anger

When a woman finally comes to terms with her depressed state, her psychic energy is now freed to effectively handle depression's cousin: anger. For women who have not learned to express anger outwardly, the help of a support group, a trusted, supportive, and empathic friend, or a therapist can aid the needed catharsis. Anger can be verbally expressed in any number of ways: "Why was I so stupid that I couldn't see this coming?" "I hate him for hurting me and the kids." "Why did I allow him to blame me for his stupid affairs, when he was the one who jumped into the sack with those bimbos!" "How could I have married such an uncaring, insensitive, passive-aggressive imbecile?"

Anger vented in the privacy of one's own company has a very different outcome from anger vented directly at the target of our aggression. When we express anger toward a former spouse directly, we cannot do so without encountering a serious back-lash. In the same way that the physical self fights an invasive infection, when the psychological self comes under attack it tries to preserve itself by charging the intruder. If we allow ourselves to become drawn into a psychological and emotional battle with our former spouse, the fight can become exhausting and render us incapable of allowing the healing that can lead to recovery. Hence, before going to battle, it is wise to ask ourselves, "Is the gain going to be worth the pain?"

We can learn to vent our angry feelings in a number of positive ways. For example, excellent ways to channel pent-up anger include physical exercise, humor, going to places that accommodate primal screams, or calling a supportive friend and asking for ten minutes to vent. A unique strategy was used by one woman who was admitted to the hospital for treatment of major depression. She related that the hospital staff gave her a room to herself, two pillows and a broomstick, and she spent two hours a day for two weeks yelling angry screams of protest at her husband as she beat the pillows to a pulp! The woman said, "I even shouted cuss words at him!"

It is essential for a woman to discover healthy ways to release her anger for five important reasons: (1) If anger continues to be repressed, a clinical depression may follow on the heels of the typical symptoms of sadness that emerge in Stage Six; (2) the woman may displace her unresolved, pent-up anger toward innocent people such as her children, friends, or co-work-ers, which can have serious ramifications; (3) unresolved anger will keep her "stuck" and prevent her from moving forward in the grieving process; (4) the unresolved anger will become part of the soiled laundry that she will take into a new relationship with a person who may not be prepared to deal with it; and

(5) the release of anger is central to resolving one's state of ambivalence that keeps us connected in a love/hate relationship with the ex-partner.

As a woman's anger dissipates, so does any remaining fear that she will not be able to survive without the relationship. She then is ready to begin to enjoy her own company.

Stage Eight: Aloneness

People often avoid aloneness to escape feelings of loneliness. These people scramble to be with others in an attempt to become swept up in an illusion of togetherness that helps them feel less alone. They become "excitement junkies," working long hours and planning activities for every night of the month. They even go out with people they don't like to be around just so they can avoid being alone. They are like balloons flying high in the wind, pumped up with the air of shallow relationships that protect them from having to confront their inner feelings of emptiness and loneliness. But take the excitement away, and the balloon pops and quickly hurls to the ground to lie limp and lifeless.

When we fear being alone, we must go and be alone. We can walk alone along a quiet beach. We can take a walk by ourselves in the woods. We can sit alone on a park bench. We can stand alone in the tower of a skyscraper and see in the distance the soft sky touching the earth. We can sit alone at a window at night and view the panorama of stars and the unbounded space that extends in all directions. Being alone is a way of discovering a spirituality that connects our inner lives with the outer world—a spirituality that is the cornerstone from which we can build healthy, meaningful, intimate relationships with loved ones, friends and, if desired, a future partner.

The sacred quality of aloneness is eloquently captured in

the lessons of the Native people of North America in an inspirational book, *The Sacred Tree*:

> A sign that much work is needed in the area of personal spiritual growth is when a person dislikes being alone, and especially dislikes being alone in silence. . . . To face ourselves alone in silence, and to love ourselves because the Creator has made us beautiful are things that every developing human being needs to learn. From this position of strength, no one can put us down, and no one can lead us to do or be anything else but what we know we must do or be.[4]

During the final phase of this stage of the grieving process, when partners have stopped investing emotionally in the relationship that has ended, they are able to wean themselves away from all the unhealthy behaviors that helped ease the pain of loneliness but prevented them from getting in touch with their unique aloneness. The tranquility that comes when we get in touch with this aloneness leads us to introspection and reflection, and lets us cultivate new perspectives, new interests, and a sense of independence—all of which are essential to the development of healthy, future relationships.

Stage Nine: Acceptance

During this stage, we begin to accept fully the painful reality of our loss, let go of any residual resentment and anger that prevented us from effectively handling that loss, and adjust ourselves to the changes that have occurred by restructuring our lives and creating new realities. We are now able to be alone to enjoy our own company, and we can be with others because we want to be, not because we need to be. We can accept reality in the light of what it is, not what it should be or might have been. We can finally acknowledge: "I made the right decision, and I am looking forward to the new adventures that my life has in store for me."

We are now prepared to develop an acceptance of ourselves. We know we have succeeded if we are able to come to know ourselves honestly and deeply and are able to get in touch with our innermost thoughts and feelings without defensive disguises.

Self-acceptance, based on healthy, genuine self-awareness, not only contributes to feeling good about being in one's own company, it also prepares us for success in future relationships. As we become more authentic and share our true selves with others, with all our strengths and weaknesses, we invite them to also feel a sense of trust and safety to openly express who they genuinely are. And, as the process continues, we gain new insights that can pave the way to a deeper level of understanding of others as well as ourselves. Without trust and safety, healthy communication between two people cannot occur.

Hence, it is within the context of this new relationship with ourselves—as well as those with whom we wish to share that self—that we begin to enhance our feelings of self-esteem, which may have been severely damaged during the divorce process.

Stage Ten: Freedom

We have come to the end of one journey and the beginning of another. When the grieving has ended—though we realize we may never forget the relationship we once had—we recognize that we no longer are using it as an excuse that can prevent us from moving on with our lives. As we move beyond our grief, we become creators of our own future and are no longer prisoners of our past. We are acutely aware that we alone hold the key to freedom. And, when the door is opened and we enter, we are:

- free to be authentic and real

- free to feel the warmth of the glow of strength and vitality that has replaced the cold, formidable fears of the past

- free to become all that we are capable of becoming

- free to accept and bear the consequences of our mistakes as well as our accomplishments

- free to forgive ourself and our ex-partner for the roles we played in the marital rupture

- free to be responsible for ourselves and our future choices

- free to be as comfortable with ourselves as we are with those about whom we care

- free to trust in our ability to love and be loved

- free to understand that there is no contradiction between loving oneself and loving another.

And, when we open the door to freedom, we are free to courageously admit that we are as apprehensive as we are eager to face the journey that lies ahead.

STRATEGIES FOR MOVING BEYOND GRIEF

When a relationship ends, there are a variety of strategies that can be used to help ease the predictable pain that emerges as you progress toward recovery. Though your journey will be unique, and it is important that you use those methods that feel comfortable to you, the following list suggests a number of possibilities from which to choose.

Take yourself seriously. Don't deny the reality of your feelings. The stages of grieving are delayed if you don't get in touch with how you feel and confront those feelings authentically.

Spend more time in the here-and-now. During crisis, some people stay stuck in the past, while others can think of nothing but the future. The past is over and cannot be changed; the future is yet to come and cannot be predicted. By living more in the here-and-now, we become less threatened by what has happened to us and less anxious about what is going to happen to us. And we free ourselves to experience, with heightened awareness, our feelings and thoughts in the present moment.

Affirm yourself. Self-affirming, positive mental energy, empowers us. It helps us become optimistic even when things around us look grim. Tell yourself several times a day, "I am a worthwhile person" or "I can handle this situation."

Establish healthy boundaries. Remember, when there are children involved, just because you are getting a divorce doesn't mean you are ending the relationship with an ex-husband. When connecting with an ex-partner, or other members of the family constellation, be aware of both the nourishing and toxic elements inherent in those contacts. Ensure that you reach out, and others reach in toward you, only as far as it is emotionally healthy to do so. Give yourself permission to set limits so that you are not manipulated or controlled by others. And, particularly during the early stages of the grieving process—a time when you may feel quite vulnerable—establishing healthy boundaries likely will prevent you from becoming co-dependently entangled in relationships.

Use guided imagery to take you to a safe place when you feel fearful, threatened or stressed. Conjure up an image of a place where you can go that is comfortable for you. It can be by a brook, in a garden, on the beach at the ocean, or any other visualization that feels safe. Take in, with all your senses, the experience of your safe place. Do this before you sleep at night or during the day. Always use the same image to reduce your stress.

Have a friend tape a relaxation exercise for you to use when you feel stressed. A voice other than your own can be a very soothing and reassuring sound. The basic steps for relaxation can be found in most stress management books.

Get enough sleep. If you are having trouble sleeping, go to bed at the same time each night and get up at the same time each morning. If you awake during the night, tell yourself, "I will save, until a specific time tomorrow, those concerns that are keeping me awake tonight." Then spend time the next day considering the issues. You probably will discover that the conflicts that create anxiety during the night are far less threatening the next day.

Don't go to bed immediately after eating dinner. And don't use sedatives to get to sleep, because there is a danger of overdose, and, over time, sedatives lose their power, requiring greater dosages to achieve the same effect. Sleeping pills should be used only under the supervision of a medical doctor.

Don't drink alcohol to put yourself to sleep. Though alcohol may initially help you fall asleep, after the sedative effects wear off, you probably will have difficulty staying asleep. Instead, try drinking a glass of milk the next time you have trouble falling asleep. The chemical compound tryptophan, which is found in milk, seems to help some people sleep better. Also, before going to bed, do not engage in stressful activities. Instead, use relaxation exercises or guided imagery to induce a relaxed state, or listen to soft music, or read a light novel.

Exercise daily. Some people like rigorous exercise, while others enjoy more moderate activities. Regardless of which you prefer, or whether your exercise of choice is jogging, gardening, walking briskly, swimming, cycling or aerobics, the effects of exercise on mental health (particularly increased self-concept, and reduced tension, anxiety, and depression) are clearly supported by research. Don't become a reclusive couch potato. Find a partner with whom to exercise, or join a health club or your local YWCA.

Focus on your eating habits. Like Carolyn in Chapter Four, many single people don't take time to eat properly. They eat standing at the kitchen sink and often do not eat a balanced diet. Take time to eat dinner. Put a flower on the table, eat slowly, and enjoy yourself.

Eliminate old self-defeating "tapes." Change your "have to's," "shoulds," "musts," and "oughts" to "WANTS." And try to eliminate the tendency to catastrophize. Remember, any problem that is created by human beings can be solved by human beings.

If you are feeling the "blahs" as you begin your day, dress to challenge how you feel. Wear something bright and cheerful. There is an old saying, "You are what you eat." There is also some wisdom in the adage, "You are how you look." You can't grieve all of the time; therefore, be motivated by your emotional lows to use your energy in constructive ways that work for you.

Use humor to lighten your life. Research has linked stress to many serious diseases, with some experts suggesting that stress may block the immune system, thereby rendering the individual vulnerable to a variety of illnesses. Conversely, there exists a growing body of support for the healing quality of laughter. Look for the ironies in life. Read the comic strips or watch some comic videos and LAUGH OUT LOUD. Also, learn to laugh at yourself.

Be with friends who are supportive. Don't isolate yourself. During the latter stages of the grieving process, you will want to learn to spend time alone. However, during the early phase, you may experience some feelings of loneliness that can be diminished by being with supportive friends. Don't wait for people to call you. They may be waiting for you to call them. Assert yourself to take care of your need to feel connected.

Search for a healthy balance in your life. Spiritual, mental, physical, and emotional well-being are all important to our health. When our lives feel fragmented, our feelings of wholeness can be restored if we cultivate and nurture a healthy balance in these four dimensions.

Spend time in service to others. If you are experiencing feelings of loneliness, rather than becoming an "excitement junkie," consider serving people in a soup kitchen, or offering to volunteer your services reading to the elderly or just listening to them talk. Time is a precious commodity, and it is a special gift to those who suffer. And time given in service to others helps us gain a clearer perspective of our own problems. It also provides us with both a sense of humility and pride, moves us beyond our own obsessive, narcissistic needs, and helps us feel a sense of connectedness with the world around us.

Join a support group. Parents Without Partners or a group for single adults can be a helpful source of support from others. Churches frequently have singles groups; if your church does not, you might want to start such a group. Support groups, however, are only as effective as the members who comprise them. Shop around for the group that is comfortable for you. If your grieving process becomes too difficult for you, seeking the services of a trained counselor for a brief period may prove more helpful than a support group. When symptoms subside, you can return to the group and gain more of the intended benefits it has to offer.

Delay making major decisions. Typically, when we make decisions during stressful times, our choices frequently reflect the emotional state we are experiencing. Feelings of anger, resentment, or guilt, for example, can hamper our ability to use good judgment about the issues at hand. In addition, when we are depressed, decisions are often difficult to make because our ability to concentrate and focus is diminished. Hold off on any major decisions. And consider seeking advice from a professional for decisions that are required in areas in which you have limited expertise, as, for example, financial planning.

Watch your compulsions. When we feel out of control, helpless, hurt or angry, compulsive behaviors can frequently become our only source of comfort. The process of recovery is not about stopping pain. It is not about feeling a temporary euphoria that eating and other addictive behaviors produce. It is about letting go and getting healthy. So, control your eating habits, buying sprees, and other compulsive, potentially addictive behaviors, or they will begin to control you.

Know whom to call when trouble strikes. Just as you would find a competent dentist and physician to care for physical problems, find people and organizations that you can count on when tasks extend beyond your own level of expertise. For example, while there is some wisdom in knowing how to change a tire, joining an automobile association can be helpful if you ever experience serious car problems. Also, if you remain in the family home, ask other divorced women for the name of an honest, competent repair person who can do odd jobs around the home. Retired people often will help with tasks such as fixing leaky faucets or cleaning clogged drains. These people enjoy helping and usually charge much less than professionals in the job market.

If you live in a home and fear being alone, get an alarm system. Though the more elaborate devices can be expensive, the benefit of being able to sleep securely at night often far exceeds the cost of an efficient system.

Take up a hobby. When the relationship ends, the period of singleness that follows can be an opportunity for you to develop your potential. For example, you might want to take a class in gourmet cooking or a foreign language, try to write poetry, learn to sew, improve your game of tennis or golf, or form a Bible study group. There are many alternatives from which to choose, and by involving yourself in new interests and activities, you develop self-direction, foster creativity, and begin to feel less empty, more hopeful, and more confident in yourself.

Develop your spiritual gifts. Whether or not you have a specific faith, and irrespective of how you define your Creator, the gift of prayer and self-reflection can be a powerful instrument of healing. However, this doesn't suggest passively leaving everything up to Providence. As one psychologist tells her clients, "Pray like everything is up to God, and work like everything is up to you."

Meet new people. Frequently, the friends we have during marriage no longer hold the same attraction following divorce. However, don't isolate yourself by saying, "There are no single people in this town." Imagine this: if you were to ask one other single woman, and two other single men, each to bring to a summer picnic two people of the opposite sex and one person of the same sex, and you did the same, you would have gathered together a group of sixteen people—eight men and eight women.

If you asked each of these people to bring to the next event one person of the same sex, and two people of the opposite sex, you would have sixty-four participants at your next social gathering! And, using the same strategy, when you are ready to plan a New Year's party, you will probably need a gymnasium to accommodate your 256 guests! The positive outcome of this approach is that you likely will gather together a group of very compatible people, since people tend to gravitate toward people who are similar in nature, age, and interests.

Take an assertiveness training class. Don't pay the price of being a "people-pleaser" by swallowing your negative feelings and ending up miserable. Assertiveness training will enable you to learn to express your feelings, wants, and needs and to act upon them in ways that do not violate the rights of others. Healthy assertiveness also helps foster respect for the feelings, wants, and needs of those around you. Local hospitals and community colleges sometimes offer assertiveness classes free of charge as a community service.

Learn effective time-management skills. There are many books on the market that can provide useful strategies for structuring your time more effectively. By learning to do so, you will have more time for yourself and your children. Many of the books also suggest ways to prevent feeling overwhelmed and stressed.

Begin putting money aside for time away from the daily routine. Even if you take a small amount of money out of each paycheck, in time you will have saved for a vacation alone or with your children. The vacation doesn't have to be extravagant —you can go camping with your children, or purchase a weekend package at a nice hotel. You might try to do something you have never done before, or choose an option that you were unable to do when you were married. It can be a lot of fun for the family to plan and anticipate a trip away from home. And the time away offers everyone a healthy respite from the routine of everyday life.

Delegate. The family unit is a social group, and it is vital that each child learn to become a contributing member of that group. As head of the family, a parent's role is much like that of the competent CEO: the chief executive officer delegates tasks, according to the needs of the organization and the abilities of its members, in order to be freed up to handle other important duties and major decisions. Within the family organization, delegated tasks that are age-appropriate can teach children a sense of responsibility and self-discipline. Having expectations of children also can prevent a parent, who may feel guilty about the marital rupture, from overindulging children to compensate for that guilt. Indulging a child to satisfy one's own need to be expiated from intense emotional feelings is counterproductive to the growth and development of children.

Reward yourself for the achievement of small steps toward more healthy behavior. During the early part of December at a presentation to a Parents Without Partners group, an older divorced woman commented that she was not looking forward to Christmas Eve because she always dreaded having her children and grandchildren leave later in the evening to return to their own homes. She said, "I feel very lonely when they leave, and I try to get them to stay longer than they really want to. I know I make my family feel guilty for leaving. And, when they leave, I go to bed and sulk all night. I hate seeing them come, because I feel so miserable when they go."

The presenter then asked the woman, "What is an activity that you can do at home that you really find pleasurable?" The woman was taken by surprise, but, after a moment of thought, she smiled and answered, "Sitting in a bubble bath, with a good book and a glass of wine." The presenter asked the woman if she would be willing to consider using this activity as a way of rewarding herself for not putting pressure on her family to stay longer than they wished on Christmas Eve. With a few minutes of gentle urging from members of her support group, she added, "Yes, I think I might like to try that!" As the presenter discussed the importance of developing a system of rewards for the achievement of small steps toward healthier behavior, the woman recognized that this self-nurturing activity would have an additional benefit—she'd break her old, unhealthy habit of having a "pity-party" after her family left for home.

Keep in mind that self-reinforcement can also be an effective motivational tool for reducing procrastination. We usually don't mind performing a difficult task if we know there is a reward waiting for us upon its completion.

Write a letter of goodbye to your ex-partner. This is a very difficult assignment; however, it is an excellent activity to aid the letting-go process. List all the things in your marriage that you are saying goodbye to. For example, "Goodbye to all the times I felt misunderstood," "Goodbye to the times I felt responsible for your happiness," "Goodbye to the times I felt ashamed for needing your stamp of approval," and "Goodbye to the times I felt frustrated when you would become emotionally frozen." When you finish the letter, do not mail it. It is solely for your benefit. Put it in a safe place and read it again at another time. It will help you remember that the decision to leave was not an arbitrary, impulsive whim.

Then, you can write a "hello" letter. You can write, for example, "Hello to meeting the challenges that lie ahead," "Hello to developing a whole new circle of friends," and "Hello to developing my spiritual life." This letter will help you gain a clearer perspective of your aspirations for the future. And when you know what you want in your life, you are far more likely to achieve it.

Join a dating service. Toward the end of the grieving process, when you feel you are ready to extend your friendship network or begin a more serious monogamous relationship with a person of the opposite sex, a dating service can be an excellent vehicle for doing so. Members are usually carefully screened by the agencies. If you are divorced, for example, dating services often will not enroll you unless you have produced evidence of a divorce decree. You have a choice about whom you may want to meet, since profiles about members are available to you. Your profile also will be on record, minus your last name, phone number, and address, so that someone may also request meeting you. Agency personnel become the mediators of the process, and telephone numbers are exchanged only with the consent of members who want to meet each other. Before joining, check to be sure that professional rules for confidentiality are guaranteed. Because some dating services are more reliable than others, be an intelligent consumer of the product you purchase. Ask many questions and, when possible, inquire about the reputation of the service from others who have used it.

Before you enroll in a dating service, note this major caveat: if you enroll at a stage of the grieving process in which your self-confidence and self-esteem are low, any request that is made by you to meet someone and is rejected can cause a severe blow to your ego. Therefore, don't throw caution to the wind by prematurely joining a service of this kind until you have recovered sufficiently from your loss and resolved most of the significant issues inherent in the grieving process.

Practice random acts of kindness. Random acts of kindness are those gentle, sweet, and loving things we do for no other reason than the sheer joy of giving. Helping a person lift a heavy bag at the grocery store counter; giving someone you don't know your seat on the bus or train; putting a quarter in the parking meter when you see that it has expired—these are only a few of the many examples of spontaneous giving that can be extended to others. Acts of kindness can change how we feel about ourselves, about loving and about life:

> For in choosing to love not only those whom you have committed yourself to loving, but also those whose names, faces, and true circumstances you will never really know, you will be moved palpably, inescapably into understanding that loving and being loved is the one true human vocation. You will see yourself as an offering, generous, bountiful soul, as well as a needing human being. You will feel connected, centered, received—deeply bonded to the human stream. In giving love, you yourself will understand that we are held in the web of life—and delivered to our divine humanity—by the random acts of kindness, the love, that we give and receive.[5]

The pain of loss is a universal experience, common to all people. The grieving process, however, is uniquely different from one person to another. And, though it is not within the scope of this chapter to demonstrate its validity, it is speculated that the grieving process may be substantively different between men and women. That hypothesis will be left for future study.

This chapter has provided a grief model consisting of ten stages, as well as a number of strategies that women might implement as they recover from loss through divorce. Those who possess the courage to authentically confront the pain that shrouds the many predictable stages of the grieving process can maximize their potential for future recovery. And women who recognize the work that must be accomplished in the process, or who have already taken the journey themselves, will, without question, possess a keener understanding of, and a deeper sense of appreciation and empathy for, women who currently suffer.

6
CHILDREN AND DIVORCE

The woman was very bitter about her husband's sudden decision to leave the family and file for a divorce. She talked frequently to family members and close friends about her hurt and her anger toward him for what he had done to her and the children. One day she was speaking on the telephone to her mother while her four-year-old was playing nearby in the room. "If we're lucky," she said, "we'll never see him again."

The child absorbed every word of her mother's conversation. Later, when the family was in counseling, the child burst into tears and told the therapist, "I'm never going to see my Daddy again."

Jeff, a serious boy and more mature than his fifteen years, was very concerned about his parents' impending divorce and how it would affect the family economically. When his dad left home, Mom told the kids that money would be tight and they would all have to give up some things.

"I know what I'm going to have to do," Jeff told the therapist. "I'll quit band and soccer and get a part-time job after school. The family needs my help."

THE IMPACT OF PARENTAL DIVORCE
ON CHILDREN

Divorce is rarely a simple and painless process. When the couple has children, the ramifications of divorce are deepened and multiplied. The child's secure and familiar world is shaken, a loved parent is suddenly absent, economic support is reduced, and the future is uncertain.

Since about 60 percent of the divorces in the United States involve children, more than a million youngsters each year join the ranks of children of divorce. Nearly one in three children will see their family split by divorce before age eighteen. It is estimated that by the end of this century, between 40 and 60 percent of all children will spend part of their growing-up years in a single-parent household, many of which are being created by divorce. For black children, the figure is even higher. It is estimated that 80 percent of them will spend part of their childhood living with just one parent. Furthermore, since the divorce rate for second marriages is higher than that for first marriages, it is not uncommon for children to see their families break apart two or even three times during childhood.

The soaring divorce rate since the mid-1960s has had a profound impact on the lives of children, making divorce a common event for many and dramatically altering the course of their childhood. Indeed, divorce seems so commonplace now that card companies produce greeting cards to fit the event and its aftermath. Cards for newly single adults and children of divorce can be found on card racks, offering congratulations to the grown-ups and attempting to comfort the sad youngsters.

The purpose of this chapter is to provide readers with insights on what to expect in children's responses to divorce and to suggest some practical guidelines that can help minimize the negative effects of divorce on children. The material should be helpful not only to parents, but also to relatives, adult friends, teachers, and other professionals who work with children.

Much has been written on how the breakup of a marriage affects children and teens, as well as the methods for identifying symptoms and providing treatment for children who are having adjustment problems. It is beyond the scope of this chapter to summarize the entire range of material available on the subject. While identifying what we see as the key issues, we also encourage you to continue to seek understanding through additional reading and consultation with professionals who are trained to work with children.

When divorce disrupts a family, the relationships between parents and children are often changed, as we try to cope with our own stresses and re-order our lives. Because of these changes, the ability of the family to fulfill its critical functions of child rearing and child protection may be weakened.

It is the rare child who does not experience at least short-term problems when parents divorce. Many children suffer negative effects for longer periods of time, carrying into their own adulthood the scars of this traumatic disruption in family life. The professional journals are filled with studies that show most children are fearful, sad, and angry about their parents' divorce. Many exhibit behavior problems at home and at school, have lower self-esteem, and have higher levels of anxiety and depression. Some children feel guilty, erroneously concluding that they were responsible for the divorce because of their "bad behavior." They may also feel ashamed and humiliated because their family is no longer like the intact families of their friends.

Even in stable and happy families, children often say their greatest fear is that Mom and Dad will divorce. They fear becoming a victim in a situation over which they have no control. In cases where the family situation is chaotic and it is apparent to the child that the parents are not getting along, the reasons for the divorce may be more understandable, but the results are no less painful for the child.

In the opinion of some professionals, the breaking of the family unit through divorce may be more difficult for children to deal with psychologically than the loss of a parent through death. While death and divorce both bring about major changes in families, two key components of grief—sorrow and anger—are expressed differently according to which event brought an end to the marriage. The consequences for children of divorce are often more serious.[1]

Death is rarely brought about through choice by a parent; divorce is. Death is final; on the other hand, many children fantasize about reversing divorce and bringing back the absent parent. When death strikes a family, the rituals of grieving and the support of others usually help children through the crisis. In divorce, however, the children may experience the shame, isolation, and lack of support that parental breakup often engenders. In *Second Chances: Men, Women, and Children a Decade After Divorce,* the pioneering ten-year clinical study of the impact of divorce on families, Judith S. Wallerstein and Sandra Blakeslee noted that fewer than 10 percent of the children they studied had any adult speak to them sympathetically as the divorce unfolded.[2]

At the five-year point in their study, Wallerstein and Joan Berlin Kelly reported that more than half the children they interviewed were distraught over their parents' decision to divorce, and less than 10 percent were relieved.[3] The separation and divorce process was the most stressful period in their lives, evoking shock, fear, and grief. And while the comforting presence of a parent is normally enough to reassure a child during other types of traumas like natural disasters, the paradox of divorce for the child is that the disruption is *initiated by the parent.* This can also have the effect of undermining the child's trust in his or her caretaker.

There is some evidence that boys and girls respond differently to their parents' divorce and subsequent family restructuring. One longitudinal study showed that parental divorce had more adverse long-term effects for boys. However, if custodial mothers remarried, this change caused more behavior problems for the daughters than for the sons. It appears that boys respond more positively to the presence of a male in the household.[4]

After studying the adjustment of children in different custody arrangements, one researcher concluded that girls who live with their mothers and boys who live with their fathers after divorce generally have fewer adjustment problems. "Children in the custody of the same-sex parent, father-custody boys and mother-custody girls, were better adjusted than children in the custody of the opposite-sex parent." However, the author cautions that the study's findings may not apply in all situations.[5]

Other studies have shown that the effects of parental divorce continue to have an impact on the children when they reach adulthood. When children of divorce become young adults, many still regard their parents' divorce as an ongoing influence in their lives. They may be unable to shake the vivid memories of the family rupture and the feelings of sadness, resentment, and deprivation associated with it.

Various studies have shown that young women who were children of divorce often have more difficulty forming healthy, lasting relationships with men. These young women may feel anxiety about leaving their mothers. They are more likely to divorce as adults than are women who grew up in intact families. Adult children of divorce seem to have a strong need for stability and structure, yet have more problems maintaining relationships. Support groups for adult children of divorce have grown in popularity as these men and women struggle to heal the hurts of the past.

While there is general agreement that children from divorced families show more behavior problems, it is difficult to sort out the origin of the problems. Some researchers believe that parental conflict before divorce can be as harmful to children as the eventual breakup. Sociologist Andrew Cherlin's study of data on more than 18,000 British and American children showed that a substantial portion of what is usually considered the effect of divorce on children is visible before parents separate. For a child, growing up in a family where serious problems exist makes normal development difficult. The study concludes that much of the effect of divorce on children can be predicted by examining the conditions that existed before the separation occurred. At least as much attention needs to be paid to what goes on in troubled, intact families as to the trauma children suffer after parents separate.[6]

In their book *Divided Families: What Happens to Children When Parents Part* Cherlin and Frank Furstenberg suggest that the Wallerstein study exaggerates the prevalence of long-term problems in children of divorce. They note that all of the problems that emerged after the breakup were blamed on the divorce:

> We do not doubt that many young adults retain painful memories of their parents' divorce. But it doesn't necessarily follow that these feelings will impair their functioning as adults. Had their parents not divorced, they might have retained equally painful memories of a conflict-ridden marriage.[7]

However, some situations can exacerbate the harmful effects of divorce on children. If we lie to our children and withhold information about the breakup, we create more anxiety for the children and undermine their trust. Wallerstein and Kelly found that four-fifths of the youngest children they studied were not provided with either an adequate explanation of the situation or assurance of their continued care. "In effect, they awoke one morning to find one parent gone."[8]

A parent who casts the children in the role of spy and informant on the ex-spouse puts the children in an uncomfortable and stressful position. Furthermore, the divorce is harder on children if a third party is involved, such as Dad having a live-in girlfriend. Children may also be at a disadvantage if the parents live

a considerable distance apart, making frequent visitation difficult. Parents may even squabble over who should drive and how
far.

Children of divorce, particularly in cases of joint custody,
may feel they have no permanent home as they are shuttled back
and forth between parents. They become, in effect, little "bag
people." As common as divorce is today, for many children it
still carries a stigma. They may feel embarrassed, different, and
deprived, envious of other children who have both parents at
home. Or, with years of practice, they may become insufferably
manipulative children, skilled in the art of having all adults meet
their real or imagined needs.

AGE-RELATED RESPONSES TO PARENTAL
SEPARATION AND DIVORCE

When parents divorce, children lose something that is fun-
damental to their development—the family structure. The family
"comprises the scaffolding upon which children mount succes-
sive developmental stages, from infancy into adolescence. It supports their psychological, physical, and emotional ascent into
maturity. When that structure collapses, the children's world is
temporarily without supports."[9]

Children of divorce lose not only the stability of a family
structure, they also lose the mom or dad they used to know. As
the adults respond to the catastrophic changes in their lives, they
may move into depressive states, which reduces their energy for,
patience with, and availability to their children. Despite a
mother's best intentions, she may not be capable of being the
same person emotionally after separation as she was prior to
separation.

Children at different ages react differently to the collapse of
the family unit. The nature and intensity of a child's response to
parental divorce depend, in large part, not only on the child's

level of understanding but also on the psychological and emotional needs at his or her stage of development. While parental divorce at each stage presents risks to the child's healthy adjustment, those close to the child—parents, relatives and teachers—can seek to understand the child's reactions and can take steps to minimize the negative effects.

A helpful way to look at the different stages of growth and development is in the following groupings: babies and toddlers, two-year-olds, pre-schoolers, six-to-eight-year-olds, nine-to-twelve-year-olds, and teenagers. By taking a closer look at the needs and typical responses of children at each stage, we can gain a better understanding of how parental divorce affects them, at least initially.

However, it is important to understand that the long-term effects of divorce on children cannot be predicted from how they react at the time of separation. The behavior patterns may shift with each developmental stage. Some research has shown that some of the children who seemed most disturbed by the divorce initially turned out fine ten years later, while problems surfaced much later for some of those who seemed least troubled at the outset.[10]

Babies and Toddlers

We may have the mistaken notion that very young children have no sense of what's happening when parents separate or divorce. But babies and toddlers, particularly in the period between ten and fourteen months of age, rely on predictable patterns in their lives. They have learned to trust what is familiar to them—the people, the settings, the routines that are part of their lives. They fear separation from those who nurture and care for them, and they are fearful of strangers who enter their world.

When parents separate or divorce, the child at this age is acutely aware of the absence of one parent. Half of the child's world has changed. Yet, at this preverbal stage, the child can't articulate this awareness or ask questions about a parent's absence. In the young child's continuing effort to have needs met for physical care, security, and nurturing, he or she can only respond to what remains unchanged. The baby or toddler doesn't wait for the absent parent to reappear. Furthermore, he or she has not yet learned to miss Daddy when he's no longer around or to mourn his absence.

Mothers who are suffering the painful effects of separation or divorce may turn to their babies to have their emotional needs met. The baby becomes the mother's whole world, the focus of all her energies, and the main source of meaning in her life. She may feel she cannot leave her child in the care of anyone else and may take the baby with her everywhere she goes. Yet this sudden shift in the young child's familiar routine can exacerbate the disruption of divorce on the baby's life. What he or she needs most is maintenance of a normal routine and the avoidance of anything that upsets the child's world even more. Letting the child stay at home in a familiar setting with a trusted caregiver might help.

Two-year-olds

By the age of two years, the normal child has developed a sense of trust in parents and has progressed to the stage of being able to have an actual relationship with those close to him or her. The two-year-old may feel quite possessive toward parents and have a sense of ownership of them. For the two-year-old who feels that "Daddy is mine," the father's sudden absence from the home will cause the child to suffer a real loss. In this situation, the child may regress in his or her behavior, act out in inappropriate ways, and become more dependent, clinging, and possessive.

If the two-year-old exhibits outrageous, regressive behavior, it is important for the parents to set limits and to maintain a consistent system of discipline when the child exceeds those limits. The tendency of parents in a divorce or separation is to become more lenient with their children in an attempt to "make up" for the disruption they've caused in the child's life. This can be a mistake, as children of all ages need reasonable limits on their behavior and the assurance that responsible adults are in charge of their world, however changed it may be.

Three- to five-year-olds

The three- to five-year-old child in a family that has been split by separation or divorce is the one who is most often confused and frightened by the situation. The child's world, once safe and secure, is now threatened. The child at this age experiences great stress and has many fears: "Since Daddy's gone, will he stop loving me? Will Mommy leave, too? Has something bad happened to Daddy? Is he okay? What if something happens to Mommy? Who will take care of me?"

Perhaps the child's greatest fear at this age is abandonment. Separation anxiety may resurface, and the child may become clinging, vigilant, and protective of the custodial parent. The preschooler may worry constantly about the parent's safety and may be reluctant to leave Mommy. However, it's important in this situation for the child to continue attending activities like nursery school or kindergarten. If the child protests and acts out, this can be particularly difficult for the mother to manage. It's helpful to explain the situation to teachers and caregivers and seek their cooperation and assistance.

Furthermore, children in this age group may regress in their behavior, clinging to formerly forgotten security blankets or toys, or wetting their pants.

The preschooler whose parents separate needs the assurance that Daddy is alive and well and still loves his child. Since the mother may avoid talking about the father, the child may think he is dead or has abandoned them for good. A photo of Daddy in the child's bedroom can be comforting. Marking the calendar for the next visit to Daddy and counting down the days will help make his existence more concrete for the child.

Women with intense negative feelings about their former partners will undoubtedly find it difficult to talk positively about their fathers to the children. However, it is critical that young children be reassured that Daddy still loves and cares for them and that having failed in some way as a husband does not mean he is a bad father. As the incident at the beginning of the chapter illustrates, mothers need to be aware of what they say about the father in the child's presence. While mothers have a legitimate need to voice their feelings about their former partners, take care not to increase the anxiety and insecurity your children may already be experiencing.

Mothers of young children may find it helpful to periodically look in a mirror, so to speak, to see themselves as their children see them. Do the children see irritability and anger in Mom? Do they see constant stress, or a mother who is dealing with the situation calmly and confidently? How we cope with divorce or separation will certainly affect our children and be reflected in their behavior. If they perceive only our weakness and our need, they may begin trying to parent us.

In general, parents can help their young children cope with a parental breakup by recognizing their need for more love, time, and attention during this difficult period. The children need to feel they are still important to the parents—and always will be—regardless of the state of the marriage.

Six- to eight-year-olds

For children of this age, divorce brings profound sadness and feelings of loss. The years between six and eight are usually times of warm relationships with parents and a sense of pride in the family. When separation or divorce occurs during this period, the child typically feels cheated of his or her rights as a member of a family. Even if family life prior to the separation was flawed, and the child's relationship with Dad was imperfect, the child tends to idealize what has been lost. The child may feel that the split is supremely unfair and that more should have been done to prevent it. This is also the age when the child fantasizes about getting the parents back together and may actually initiate strategies to restore the family unit.

The child may be able to understand and deal with the facts of the situation, but may be incapable of coping with the emotional consequences. For example, he or she may have difficulty expressing anger toward the departed parent—usually the father—assuming that being angry would destroy the love between them. The child who is extremely resentful about the breakup may then direct resentment toward the mother, who finds this hard to understand. "Their father is the one who left the family; why aren't they angry with him?" she wonders. Often the child may feel torn between loyalty to each parent.

Even when children of this age see the departed parent through regular visitation, it is not unusual for them to be unhappy wherever they are. They recall and miss the "good old times" when the family was whole. It seems that they will not find peace and contentment unless the parents get back together. The pictures drawn by children in this age group graphically depict both physical separation and the fantasies of life under the same roof once again.

Nine- to twelve-year-olds

While children in this age group experience some of the same intense feelings about divorce as younger children do, the preteens seem better able to understand the situation and to cope with the changes it brings. Most are more direct about expressing and focusing their anger.

Nine- to twelve-year-olds typically have a strong sense of right and wrong and tend to be moralistic. They may openly make judgments about their parents' behavior. Dad may be doing something the child regards as morally wrong, like seeing another woman. For the child who loves Dad, this creates painfully ambivalent feelings.

If these children perceive one parent as being more responsible for the breakup of the marriage, they may, in their own way, try to punish that parent. This can be particularly hard on mothers who have custody of their preteens. Girls may sulk and become uncooperative. Boys may become disobedient and create discipline problems for their mothers. "If I'm so bad," the boy may reason, "Dad will have to come back." This can add to the mother's stress and make her feel less competent as a parent.

Children of this age are very conscious of money and how it affects the family's lifestyle. They often have deep fears about the financial impact of a divorce, and they may blame one parent or the other for creating economic hardship. It's helpful for the custodial parent to share with the preteens, in a straightforward way, information about finances: "The support check didn't arrive yet, so we can't go shopping." However, avoid catastrophising: "If your father doesn't send that check, we're going to end up on the street!" And resist the tendency to put the children in the middle to negotiate for more money from Dad. (One mother always dressed her children in their shabbiest clothes for their visit to their father to impress upon him their dire financial condition.)

Preteens are often super detectives. They will try to get to the bottom of the mystery of their parents' breakup, searching for clues to parental behavior. They will seek out evidence that Dad is seeing another woman or Mom is carelessly spending the family's money.

It is important for parents of preteens to tell them the truth about an impending separation or divorce. Not to do so can seriously damage the children's trust. The parents *together* should present the facts of the situation simply and directly and answer the children's questions without placing blame.

Teenagers

In many respects, parental divorce during the teen years presents the most difficult problems. Young people coping with hormonal changes, identity crises, and a daily array of choices about behavior are suddenly faced with the changes a family breakup brings. This comes at a time when what they need most at home is stability and security. Consequently, teens may try to replace their own family with the family of a friend, where they can find a measure of safety and security. Or they may turn even more to the comfort and familiarity of the peer group. Don't be surprised if your teen spends less and less time at home.

This is also the time for young people to begin to break away from the family and to establish their own connections, values, and lifestyles. While this is a natural and usually healthy tendency, we need to be aware of our teens' activities and set realistic limits and guidelines for their behavior. Parents coping with the stresses of divorce may fail to pay attention to their teens or may unwisely become too permissive and fail to provide needed controls.

The timing of a family breakup during a child's teen years may seem bitterly ironic to the adolescent. A parent is leaving home at the very time that adolescents are preparing for their own leave-taking as they move toward maturity and independence. It's as though the roles have been reversed.

Complicating the situation further for the young person is the changed relationship with parents that divorce may bring and any altered behavior on the part of parents that teens perceive as adolescent. Teens may be distressed when suddenly single parents take on a new lifestyle, try to look younger, begin dating, and become sexually active. A parent may begin relating to the teen more as a friend at a time when the young person really needs a parent. The generation gap is narrowed, and parents begin to look like competitors. It's not surprising that teens in this situation would feel deserted and betrayed by their parents at a time when the adolescents most need adult support.

Some pragmatic teens, like Jeff at the beginning of the chapter, respond to parental divorce by suddenly growing up and taking charge. They feel responsible for keeping the family functioning and take on adult roles that rob them of their teen years. This could mean taking a job, neglecting social life and recreational activities, and even dropping out of school. We may unwittingly reinforce this shift in roles by placing adult expectations on our teens and turning to them in the absence of our marriage partner.

One mother, many years after her divorce, realized that she had been expecting her son to take on a father role in dealing with his two younger sisters. When asked, once again, to talk to his sisters about a problem they were having, he blurted out: "I'm tired of always having to be the father in this family!"

When a parental split places economic hardships on the family, teens often suffer a direct and immediate impact. Spending may be curtailed for all but absolute necessities, and the teen may have to contribute to the family income with a part-time job. Such changed circumstances can cause bitter reactions from teens, who may see themselves as economic hostages of the divorce. Some respond by engaging in crafty manipulation of each parent in order to obtain new clothes, gifts, or extra spending money. They may watch closely how each parent spends money and report this back to the other parent, which can spark further conflicts between the former spouses.

This is the age when children of divorce show the greatest resistance to visiting the absent parent. It is common for teens in any family to avoid doing things with their parents. In split families teens may resist even more being dragged away from their own activities to visit with the parent who left home. As custodial parent, you may be cast in the uncomfortable role of mediator, trying to make arrangements or offer explanations. It's better to leave the negotiating to the other parent and the teen, in order to avoid being caught in the middle of a conflict.

HELPING CHILDREN COPE

While the breakup of their parents' marriage is a traumatic event for most children regardless of age, steps can be taken to minimize the negative effects and to help them adjust to an altered family life. Wallerstein and Kelly concluded from their study that when children understand their parents' divorce as a serious and carefully considered remedy for an important problem, purposefully and rationally undertaken, the child is better able to cope with the family rupture. Conversely, when the divorce is unplanned, undertaken impulsively, or pursued in anger or guilt, the child's capacity to cope is severely burdened.[11]

How children recover from parental divorce depends not only on their individual nature and coping skills, but also on their ongoing relationship with their parents as well as their parents' relationship with each other. Children do better if parents can keep open their communications with each other and can ensure that their children's needs are being met. A child's adjustment to the changed family structure will be more positive if the family can continue to function in a way that meets the child's needs and provides stability and security.

Many professionals who have studied children of divorce agree that the child's relationship with the custodial parent and how that parent functions is a critical factor in the child's adjustment. Though statistics vary from state to state, in the majority of divorces mothers retain sole physical custody of their children.

Hence, most of the day-to-day responsibility for their well-being will rest on the mother's shoulders, while she may be dealing with her own distress and negative feelings about the divorce. Her burdens are increased if she doesn't receive needed financial support from the father, or if he fails to maintain regular contact with the children and stay involved in child rearing. (Several surveys have revealed the surprisingly low level of contact that divorced fathers have with their children, many of whom reported they had not seen their fathers in a year or more.)

Therapists and other professionals in child development offer suggestions like the following to help both parents lessen the pain and confusion that divorce can cause their children:

- Once the decision to separate/divorce has been made, the parents together should tell the children, in an age-appropriate fashion, the truth about the rupture in their relationship and that they see the decision as a solution. If the children are not close in age, talk further with them individually.

- Assure the children that they are not responsible for their parents' conflicts and the breakup of the marriage.

- Reassure the children that they are loved and will be cared for and that the custodial parent is primarily responsible for them.

- Encourage the children to ask questions and express their concerns. Help them to be prepared for what will happen next and how the changes in the family will affect them.

- Reassure them that they will have ongoing access to the noncustodial parent through regular visits and outings.

- Respect the privacy of their time with the other parent; avoid prying with questions about the ex-partner or making derogatory remarks about him/her.

- Try to keep the various elements of the child's environment as stable as possible—school, playmates, rituals, routine activities.

- Move quickly to establish new family rituals when old ones can no longer be observed, or if Dad's absence makes the situation uncomfortable. (For example, if Dad always cooked dinner on the night Mom worked late, that could become the night of the week that Mom and the kids go out for pizza.)

- As the custodial parent, try to give each child at least fifteen minutes of individual personal time each day. Use the time to listen to your child, rather than lecturing or venting your own feelings.

- Don't force the children to choose which parent to ask to an event because the parents are uncomfortable if both attend. When possible, both parents should attend school functions, club activities, athletic events, parent-teacher conferences, and so on. It will help the children if both parents show support and cooperation in achieving goals for their children. However, establish and keep boundaries between yourself and your ex-spouse; don't create the impression that you're still married, or send the children mixed messages about reuniting.

- Provide a permanent living space for the child to use when visiting the noncustodial parent. Children need a space to call their own. Let them take along a favorite toy, blanket, or other possession.

- Inform other adults in the child's life (such as relatives, family friends, teachers, pastor, pediatrician) about the divorce so they can act as a support network for the child. However, talk privately with these individuals to determine their attitudes about divorce. You'll want some assurance that they won't say something to your child that increases anxieties and fears, like the comment made by a clergyman that Dad was going to hell for leaving Mom for another woman.

- Show your children that you have a life of your own that includes friends, interests, and activities. This is especially important for mothers who may have the tendency to make their children their whole world after a divorce.

DANGER SIGNS

As discussed earlier, most children will show some changes in attitude and behavior when they learn of the breakup in their parents' marriage. Such reactions are normal and predictable. By expecting and understanding these effects in otherwise normal children, parents can relieve some of their own guilt and anxiety and can help their children adjust to the new family situation. Over time, most children heal. However, in some cases, marital dissolution can have a deeper and more serious effect on children, who may require professional help in coping and moving ahead in their growth and development.

Parental divorce may plunge a child into a deep and long-term depression, as contrasted with occasional and temporary periods of sadness and moodiness. In the Wallerstein and Kelly study, one-third or more of the children showed a variety of acute depressive symptoms five years after the divorce. The depressed children were having problems with school and social adjustment, and many were acting out inappropriately. Their symptoms included sleeplessness, restlessness, difficulty in concentrating, deep sighing, feelings of emptiness, play inhibition, compulsive overeating, and somatic complaints of various kinds.[12]

Watch for significant variations in your children's normal patterns, such as changes in eating and sleeping habits, a depressed mood, frequent irritability, a high level of anger or anxiety, uncharacteristically poor schoolwork, withdrawal from friends, delinquent behavior and so on. The child may refuse, or be unable, to talk with the parents about what is troubling him or her. If such changes persist and are atypical of the child's usual behavior, you may need to get your child professional help from a therapist and/or arrange for participation in a children-of-divorce support group.

A number of studies have documented the positive outcomes of group intervention programs for children who are struggling with the effects of their parents' divorce. Preventive intervention programs, which have increased in number around the country in recent years, help children of divorce cope with their problems, increase their self-esteem, reduce feelings of isolation, and find support. The groups, which are typically school-based and geared to elementary school children, use a variety of activities like role-playing, drawing pictures, and group discussion. Children are encouraged to share their feelings with their parents, and parents are encouraged to become more involved in helping their children heal.

THE ROLE OF TEACHERS

Teachers can be particularly helpful to children of divorce if the teachers are informed about the situation, as school provides continuity when the child's home life is disrupted. However, even concerned and compassionate teachers may have negative expectations for these children and may become vigilant for symptoms they have been told to expect. They may then end up neglecting the positive dimensions of a child's behavior, skills, and capacities in the school setting, thereby inadvertently contributing to the child's maladjustment.

Numerous studies have shown that teacher expectation affects how much children learn. Research has also confirmed that teachers seem to expect that children of divorce will have poorer social adjustment and be less able to cope with stress as a result of parental divorce.

In one study, thirty teachers looked at a videotape depicting the social behavior of an eight-year-old boy, rated him on personality traits, and predicted his behavior in different situations. Half the teachers were told that the boy was from a divorced home, and half were told that he came from an intact home. The teachers who thought the boy was a child of divorce rated him as less happy, less well-adjusted, less able to cope with stress, and less socially skilled. The teachers who were told the boy was from an intact home did not rate him as negatively.[13]

Certainly, children of divorce are at risk for developing adjustment problems, as much of the research cited in this chapter indicates. But we need to realize that the same bias that influences educators might also affect parents as we respond to the needs of our children at this transitional time. Being aware of potential problems and being prepared to respond to them are not the same as developing negative, self-fulfilling prophecies about our children. A more positive approach for parents, teachers, and others who interact with children of divorce is to focus on hopeful outcomes. This could include employing such approaches as:

- Moving beyond a day-to-day survival mode to a more forward looking approach by talking with children about their accomplishments and their dreams and aspirations for the future;

- Providing ongoing reassurance for younger children by telling stories with animal characters who face sad, scary times but find love, security, and a bright future;

- Recognizing and acknowledging the healthy and successful times the child has and rewarding the child's effort more than the outcome;

• Not allowing the child's emotional stress to be an acceptable excuse for inappropriate behavior. (We don't serve children well by letting them learn they are not going to be held accountable for their choices and behaviors.)

THE DIVORCE DILEMMA

In light of what we know about the negative effects of divorce on children, and given the desire of most parents to act in the best interests of their children, the perennial question arises: Is it better for the kids when parents stay in a bad marriage or when they divorce?

The answer is neither simple nor clear-cut. There is no hard evidence nor general agreement that divorce is either more or less damaging to children than is an unhappy marriage. Some children will fare better in a peaceful, single-parent home, while for others, divorce may be worse than living in an unhappy, intact family. In family situations where children are exposed to severe physical and verbal abuse, divorce and subsequent custody by the nonabusive parent is likely to bring more safety and security to the child's life. Some experts contend that persistent fighting and discord between the parents has a more deleterious effect on a child than does divorce. The Cherlin study, referred to earlier in the chapter, shows that children can suffer as much from parental conflict in intact families as from the effects of divorce.

Another study of the effects of marital disruption on children's behavior confirmed that divorce was, indeed, associated with a higher incidence of behavior problems, such as depression/withdrawal, antisocial behavior, and impulsivity. However, the study also showed that the negative effects were lower if the children lived with the same-sex parent following divorce, or maintained a good relationship with one or both parents. The report of the study also concluded: "Marital conflict in intact homes, especially if persistent, appears to be as harmful as disruption itself."[14]

When facing a decision about divorce, it is important to keep in mind that children may view their parents' relationship quite differently from the way we as adults view it. The children's needs and interests are not the same as those of the parents, and children experience family life in their own unique way. Many couples today expect to find emotional gratification and personal fulfillment in their marriages. When one partner seeks divorce because he or she feels bored or unfulfilled in marriage, the divorce will not necessarily benefit the children. What contributes to a parent's happiness may shatter a child's well-being. It may be very difficult for a child to understand how the parents' marriage can be so bad as to break up the family, or how a divorce will make things better.

The Wallerstein and Kelly study showed that only a few of the children thought their parents were happily married, yet most preferred the unhappy marriage to the divorce. While many of them had lived for years in an unhappy home, they did not see the divorce as a solution to their unhappiness, nor did they greet it with relief.[15]

A child psychiatrist who has studied the effects of divorce on children has concluded:

> My own belief is that the effects on the children should be one of the considerations in the divorce decision, but not the major one. The major determinant should be whether the parents feel that there is enough pain in their relationship to warrant its being broken. However, in addition to considering the frustrations and privations each will suffer following the separation and divorce, they should also try to imagine the effects on their children. They should not just assume that their children will be better off if they divorce, or that whatever will be best for them will automatically be best for the children as well.[16]

In a country-western song popular several years ago, a male singer wailed plaintively about a beautiful, idyllic love affair that a married man had to abandon "for the sake of the children." Some marriage partners still make decisions like that. Others decide, for a variety of reasons, that divorce is their only option, but are concerned, nevertheless, about the impact the action will have on the children. They may agonize over the timing of the divorce—that is, at what age will divorce have the least negative impact on children?

While there is rarely a "good" time for a divorce, some professionals believe that the younger the children are, the less likely they are to suffer long-term, negative effects. Before the age of three years, children have no permanent verbal memory and are not likely to remember the events surrounding the divorce. When parental divorce occurs before children reach age five, girls appear to recover from most ill effects within two years. Boys seem to take longer to bounce back, especially if the mother attempts to place her son in the absent father's role. (However, as discussed earlier, studies show some children, particularly girls, experience latent adjustment problems related to their parents' divorce years later after reaching adulthood.)

However, not all experts agree that the younger the child, the less the damage. In fact, the younger the children are at the time of the divorce, the less apt the father may be to remain involved in their lives and be available to them through all their developmental stages. (One mother, who divorced when her children were young, said that despite frequent visits, their father "never really knew them" as they grew up.) Some professionals believe that older children, who have more sophisticated reasoning ability, can understand and accept divorce easier than their younger siblings can.

Furthermore, the younger the children are at the time of the divorce, the longer they are exposed to the loss of one parent in the home. The older the children are at the time of separation, the longer they will have had the beneficial effects of living with both parents. However, putting off divorce until the children are older is not necessarily recommended, as living in an unhappy home can also be detrimental to children.

At any rate, several researchers have found that, over time, age and sex factors seem to be less relevant to positive outcomes for the children than are other factors. In their five-year follow-up of the families they studied, Wallerstein and Kelly found that other components, in varying combinations, had a major effect on the children's recovery from divorce. These included such factors as: the extent to which the parents had been able to resolve and put aside their conflicts and angers; the custodial parent's handling of the child; the child's ongoing relationship with the noncustodial or visiting parent; the range of personality assets and deficits that the child brought to the divorce; the availability to the child of a supportive human network; and the absence of continuing anger and depression in the child.[17]

It is well to keep in mind that separation, divorce, and post-divorce involve a complex process that proceeds in stages over time. For most children, the strong reactions and intense stress they experience initially when their parents decide to split will gradually lessen as the new family situation stabilizes. Much of the child's satisfactory adjustment depends on the nature of the new family unit and how it is achieved.

Certainly a major factor in determining how children feel about themselves and how they adjust to life after divorce is the quality of the mother-child relationship. When the mother is able to recover emotionally from the trauma of marital rupture and build a new life for herself, she is better able to help her children. The next chapter offers insights into the recovery process, barriers that may prevent a woman from rebuilding her life after divorce, and guidelines for healthy adjustment.

７

REBUILDING YOUR LIFE
AFTER DIVORCE

When Rita married, she put her career on hold to devote herself to the roles of wife, homemaker, and mother. Eventually, marital conflict and years of unhappiness led her to the decision to leave the marriage.

The day came when she faced the difficult task of explaining to her teenage children why she wanted a divorce. Her son, stunned and dismayed by the news, responded: "Mom, now your life is over!"

Like Rita's son, those who see a women's life as viable only in the context of marriage will, indeed, regard it as over when the marriage dissolves. The woman herself may feel adrift and rudderless as her roles and functions change, her social life dries up, and she suddenly must operate as a single person in what is still largely a couples' world.

The dissolution of a marriage, difficult and painful as it is, is but half the process. The journey does not end with the divorce decree. For those who divorce, the task of rebuilding one's life begins, and it may continue for years before the journey is complete.

In this chapter we will summarize some of the issues that women face as they strive to become autonomous and self-actualizing individuals. We will briefly look at the gender-related messages that can inhibit a woman's growth and often work against her during the divorce and rebuilding process. We will examine the ways in which different women respond to marital breakup and highlight those categories of women who are particularly vulnerable to damage in divorce.

Finally, we will look at the factors that help women adjust positively to divorce, and we will offer guidelines for rebuilding life as single persons. We will hear in the words of women themselves how they made it through the trauma and disruption of divorce and what they would share with other women who are attempting to lead whole, fulfilling lives as uncoupled individuals.

ROADBLOCKS AND DETOURS

Despite the considerable advances of women since the 1970s in the arenas of work, politics, and lifestyle choices, women still find barriers to their growth and development. Their road to equality and self-determination is frequently filled with roadblocks and detours. At the outset of this book, we posed the dilemma of today's married woman as she struggles for both autonomy and intimacy in the context of changing attitudes about marriage. The divorce revolution and the alarms it has raised over the potential demise of the nuclear family provide the societal setting as the woman works out her individual drama. At stake for her is the achievement of a genuine sense of self and an integrated wholeness, without which she is unlikely to develop a healthy, interdependent, intimate relationship.

Subsequent chapters explored a number of psychological and situational conflicts that can arise in a marriage when partners' needs are not met and communication is stymied. We have seen how women often feel a conflict between a desire to meet their own needs for growth and fulfillment and the expectations of their gender roles. Women learn that asserting themselves to reach their fullest potential can pose a threat to their relationships, and they find they must manage a delicate balancing act to keep the peace.

Within themselves, many women feel a constant tug between their need for nurturing and their desire for independence. One woman's favorite tee shirt, a relic from the 1970s, expressed this touching duality: "Liberated women need love too."

We explored the ways in which communication serves different purposes for women and men. In sharing the problems they are experiencing, women look for understanding, caring, and supportive encouragement, not necessarily solutions. A women's marital dissatisfaction is often rooted in her inability to identify and communicate her unsatisifed needs to her partner.

We saw how the conflicts women experience in marriage can lead to frustrations and draw women into unhealthy behavior patterns, like "the blame game," "the should syndrome," and "the porous rock." When conflicts are not resolved, women tend to hold in their anger and bury it within themselves, sowing the seeds for depression. Chapter Four helped readers to understand depression, a serious, debilitating condition to which women are particularly vulnerable. Chapter Five examined the stages of grieving, a normal and essential process for those suffering the loss of a broken relationship. Chapter Six posed some of the issues parents face when dealing with children's responses to divorce.

Given the tug of frequently conflicting roles and expectations placed on today's woman, and the barriers she encounters on her journey to empowerment, it is not surprising to find her often stumbling, hesitating, or even giving up to forces she feels she cannot control. If she embarks on the divorce process—whether willingly or reluctantly—she will find herself continuing to grapple with these forces as she strives to emerge as a healthy and whole person ready to take control of her future.

DIVORCE AND GENDER

Whether the woman decides "enough is enough" and initiates the divorce, or her husband takes action for his own reasons, she is likely to view the dissolution of her marriage with a good deal of anxiety and ambivalence. Women often say that the thing they fear most about life as a divorced person is the pain of loneliness. For most of us, relationships and connections to others are extremely important; as women we may even define ourselves in terms of our relationships. When a marriage breaks up, a woman may feel that a part of her identity has been taken away.

Other concerns follow close behind, exacerbated by the gender-related messages that women have learned and that place them in vulnerable positions during marital breakup. Two women who have studied this problem write:

> Generally, women in divorce procedures feel terror about abandonment, confusion about legal and financial matters, ambivalence about their entitlements, fear of conflict, protectiveness over others' feelings (often to their own detriment), and fear of retaliation. This symptom picture often leads clinicians to highlight divorcing women's responses as pathological or co-dependent, whereas, in fact, their behavior reflects integration of learned gender-related messages.[1]

Such behavior patterns can lead women to make decisions in the divorce process that are not in their best interests. Even in the most amicable divorces, conflicts arise that require self-assertion and authority, traits not considered typically "feminine." If we have been socialized to avoid conflict, to be the peacemaker, to put others' needs ahead of our own, and to leave decision-making to males, we are likely to come out with the short end of the stick.

This happened to a woman we know who caved in to her husband's threats to cut the children out of his will if she insisted on receiving alimony to supplement her low wages. Typically, a woman will be willing to sacrifice what she is entitled to if her husband threatens to use the children as a wedge, such as contesting custody. In addition, it is often difficult for women to relinquish their nurturing role and sense of responsibility for the well-being of their former spouse. An example of this is the woman who, left by her husband after a long-term marriage, continued to feel responsible for nurturing him through his midlife crisis. Still another woman, who reported that she had never fought with her husband in their twenty-five years of marriage, had to learn to stand up for herself and fight for what she wanted in the divorce settlement.

Women who have learned to empathize with others and make excuses for their behavior may blame themselves for the failure of their marriage. They may even rationalize their husband's abusive behavior. One young woman was shocked when, in the midst of an argument with her husband, he threw her to the floor and began choking her. When he released her after "teaching her a lesson," she called the police. She later felt guilty about his arrest and wondered if her response had permanently damaged their relationship!

Perceptive therapists will recognize the gender-related messages and fears that we as women carry into the divorce process, as well as the societal bias that exists toward women. Through therapy, women can receive support, ego enhancement, and strategies to reduce the onset of depression after divorce. "For divorcing women, growth occurs as their entitlements are confirmed, their needs and desires are recognized, and they become able to represent their own interests."[2]

A SOLUTION WITH STRESSES

When a marriage dissolves, one or both partners typically view divorce as a solution to the problems they are experiencing

—the end to unhappiness, dissatisfaction, and conflict. They may or may not realize when they make this choice that, for most people, divorce is a stressful life change that is disruptive and emotionally draining. It is usually accompanied by dramatic changes in family structure, finances, roles and responsibilities. In some ways, life after separation and divorce often becomes more difficult than it was during marriage.

One goal of this book has been to help both men and women examine their relationships, gain insights about the conflicts they are experiencing, and seek professional counseling to heal the rifts in their relationship. We have attempted to shed light on the complex process that brings a woman to the point of deciding that divorce is an option, at least in situations where she is making the decision. We have neither advocated for nor argued against divorce but have presented the issues that women, in particular, must cope with when their marriage is dissolved. We believe that if women enter the divorce process more fully informed about the pitfalls they face, and if they possess information, support and access to resources, they are more likely to reduce the harmful effects of divorce and go on to rebuild their lives in a positive way.

As our previous discussions have indicated, divorce brings with it a number of new stresses and strains for many women. These often include a change in her economic status and concerns about her financial future, which we discussed in Chapter Three. She may become isolated socially and lose her previous social status. Further complicating her adjustment to these unfamiliar and often frightening changes may be her own ambivalence about the divorce—even if she initiated it—and her lingering feelings of attachment to her ex-spouse.

Depending on her life stage, the woman may be particularly vulnerable to the changes and pressures separation and divorce bring. If there are children in the family, she is likely to shoulder more responsibility for their care and rearing. Young mothers who are suddenly single parents may be consumed by the challenge of surviving financially, physically, and emotionally.

The woman who divorces during her middle years (35 to 55) faces her own unique stresses. If she has been primarily a homemaker, she may find herself thrust into an unfamiliar work world. Research has shown that a woman at this stage of life:

> . . . frequently suffers a deeper psychological and social dislocation than the younger woman and that she grapples with dependence on young adult children and loneliness in a youth-oriented culture, where body image and confidence about building new relationships are easily eroded with increasing age. Also, she must earn money for herself (and perhaps her children) in the context of divorce laws and a labor market that make earning an adequate income difficult."[3]

In her long-term study of divorced families, Judith Wallerstein found that older women (and older men as well) who came out of long-term marriages were alone and unhappy, they tended to lean on their children, and they faced the future with anxiety. The older women experienced less psychological change after divorce than did their younger counterparts, and they still mourned the loss of their role as wife, mother, homemaker, and nurturer. In essence, they were less apt to explore their "second chances."[4]

Who, then, is happy after divorce? Wallerstein and Sandra Blakeslee found in their ten-year follow-up interviews that for most of the former couples, one person was happier and better off—usually the one who wanted the divorce. In only 10 percent of the couples did both husband and wife build happier, fuller lives. Almost half of the women and two-thirds of the men said they had no better or worse quality of life than before the divorce. However, while they may not be totally satisfied with their current lives, 80 percent of the women and 50 percent of the men affirmed the divorce decision.[5]

ADJUSTING TO LIFE AFTER DIVORCE

If, indeed, there are winners and losers in the divorce process, what determines the outcome? A number of studies have been undertaken in an attempt to determine the factors that are likely to lead to a positive adjustment to divorce, as well as those that inhibit adjustment. While there are no definitive answers to the question of what makes adjustment more or less difficult, awareness of these factors can help women, and the therapists who work with them, to take steps to effect changes in the woman's behavior and attitudes that might lead to healthier outcomes.

Because adjustment can be measured in a number of ways and has many dimensions, definitions of adjustment vary. Gay C. Kitson offers this understanding:

> To have adjusted, a person must have sufficiently mastered the social, psychological, and economic events facing him or her that he or she is able to go about the tasks —and pleasures—of daily life without difficulty. Thus, adjustment is defined here as "being relatively free of symptoms of psychological disturbance, having a sense of self-esteem, and having put the marriage and former partner in enough perspective that one's identity is no longer tied to being married or to the former partner." Such a definition assumes that a person has been able to put enough psychological distance between himself or herself and the divorce to be able to move ahead with his or her life. This does not mean that divorce-related problems and issues will not continue to arise, but that an individual will be able to deal with these in a relatively straightforward manner.[6]

In a study of divorced couples in metropolitan Cleveland, Kitson found that adjustment problems were evident in four areas: subjective distress (as felt by the individual), lingering attachment to the ex-spouse, self-esteem, and the occurrence of illness. Lingering attachment, in particular, appeared to be the source of much of the heightened psychological distress experienced by the divorced persons. Breaking the legal bonds of a marriage is not the same as breaking the psychological bonds.

Kitson also found that some common factors that affected adjustment among all the men and women were: the presence of other negative events at the time of the divorce; who suggested the divorce; and the divorcing person's economic situation. When asked about the specific difficulties they experienced as a result of the divorce, both men and women mentioned difficulties related to "living alone" and "taking on new roles." However, women were more likely to mention problems in "adjusting to independence" and "being a single parent" as specific problems within these two areas.

On the brighter side, Kitson found that though "the majority of the subjects felt that the divorce was generally an unpleasant experience, some of the unpleasantness faded with time, and the benefits of the decision became clearer." Approximately four years after separation, most of the divorced subjects differed little in terms of psychological functioning from their married counterparts, although some still scored higher in subjective distress.[7]

In another study, a group of researchers who followed men and women for two years after marital separation found that the adults' postdivorce coping, emotional adjustment, and psychological functioning depended on an interplay of stressors and strains, personal resources, social resources, and attachment to the ex-spouse. While higher occupational and educational status enhanced adjustment for the men but not the women, the women's psychological functioning before separation strongly helped her later adjustment.

This study also found that conflict with the ex-spouse impaired both the men's and women's postdivorce adjustment. The strain of the conflict sustained a hostile, negative attachment to the ex-partner for several years after separation. However, positive attachment to the ex-spouse also impaired adjustment. On the other hand, those women who were more involved socially were less attached to their ex-spouse, were able to cope more effectively after separation, and showed less distress. The researchers concluded: "For women, a greater degree of social involvement decreases both positive and negative attachment to their ex-spouse, which in turn results in better postdivorce adjustment."[8]

Another study examined the ways recently divorced women saw their roles in the family and how these perceptions affected their adaptation to the changes divorce brings and to the restructuring of the family unit. The researchers found that the woman's adaptation to life as a single parent was affected by the meaning and value she attached to her mothering role, as well as her acceptance of a work identity. The women in the study were characterized as "traditionalist," "modifier, and "career directed." After separation, the traditionalists remained child and home centered, maintaining the prominence of their mothering role. The modifiers began to incorporate a broader set of role options, including work. The career-directed women showed less stress, did more planning for the changes, and embraced work opportunities.

As might be expected, the traditional women faced the most difficulty in reorganizing their family life structure after separation and experienced the greatest stress in adapting to single life:

> Having divorced reluctantly, they tried to maintain as many family patterns as possible. In some ways, their commitment to traditional values inhibited their ability to form new roles and structures around the altered family configuration. Many of the traditional women felt overwhelmed by their attempt to conserve their predivorce identity of full-time mother while taking outside work roles.[9]

Because the behaviors and values embedded in the wife/mother role were so critical to the self-identity of these women, many of their personal resources were engaged in coping with this loss rather than with the tasks of the restructured family's life cycle. The traditional woman's attitude toward her role as breadwinner remained negative. And although she did not alter her basic values, over time she reduced her expectations for herself in the mothering role.

The study found that the "modifiers" moved more rapidly into their new roles and gained a new sense of competency as breadwinner and decision maker. The reorganization process for the career-directed women was brief and often brought relief, giving her a new sense of autonomy. The researchers concluded that women whose role orientation resembled the traditional group were most likely to have difficulty developing new roles and probably were in most need of counseling during the divorcing period.[10]

Other studies have confirmed the positive effect that a work role can have for divorced women as they strive for new identity and accomplishment. In one study, 500 American and British managers who had separated or divorced were surveyed to determine how marital dissolution had affected their daily work activities and long-term career development. While divorce increased stress levels for both men and women, 70 percent of women surveyed said they became more involved in their work as a way to gain balance in their life. Divorce increased the women's work achievement. Also, work relationships may become more important to divorced persons as a source of support and friendship.[11]

A woman's socioeconomic status can also have a bearing on how she sees herself in relation to marriage and how this perception affects her adjustment to divorce. One researcher who studied the divorce experience of working and middle-class women noted that working-class women were more likely to define their identity as married persons. These women felt they lost their identity when the marriage dissolved. On the other hand, the middle-class women felt their marriage had inhibited their growth and development. They had begun to establish professional identity prior to the divorce and continued in their personal and professional growth after divorce. "On the other hand, working-class women directed their efforts toward developing stability and consistency in their lives to promote emotional adjustment to the divorce among their children. Working-class women discussed solving one family crisis after another and becoming emotionally stronger with each success." Both groups said they felt much better about themselves, and they showed a strong sense of determination to succeed. They regarded improvement in their identity and self-esteem as progress in their postdivorce adjustment.[12]

While a stressful life change like divorce is disruptive and disequilibrating, it can also serve as a catalyst for a woman's further growth and development. One study analyzed the adjustment and ego level of a group of women a year after divorce, utilizing the theory that ego unfolds and progresses through various stages. Taken into consideration was the individual's adaptation to and integration of stressful life events into her customary orientation toward the self and the external world. Ego level was measured by such factors as self-esteem, life satisfaction, mood disturbance, stress symptoms, and physical health. The researcher found that the women who made a successful adaptation to divorce showed a significant increase in ego level. Women who showed poor adjustment a year after divorce had regressed in their ego level.[13]

One of the conclusions of Wallerstein's ten-year study was that women undergo more psychological change than men do after divorce. She found that many women were completely different people ten years after divorce and showed striking growth in competence and self-esteem. She also observed that recovery after divorce involved a number of factors:

An adult is more likely to succeed after divorce if he or she has some history of competence, some earlier reference point to serve as a reminder of earlier independence and previous successes. For all, recovery from crisis is an active process. It can be facilitated by the luck of the draw or by a chance meeting, but it involves active effort, planning, and the ability to make constructive use of new options and to move ahead. It helps to have talent, marketable skills in a good marketplace, and social skills that catalyze support networks. The lucky ones have families and children willing and able to help and money saved up or available. Such things make it easier. But there are no guarantees of success.[14]

RESPONSES THAT HELP REBUILD

As with any crisis, the breakup of a marriage presents both threats and opportunities. The outcome, in large part, depends on how individuals respond to it. Those undergoing this major life change may feel overwhelmed by its demands for new behaviors and may face the future reluctantly with fear and uncertainty. Or, despite the disruption and anxieties divorce brings, those who go through it may recognize the opportunities it presents for positive change and new life.

While each marriage is as unique as its partners and every divorce is different, common elements and issues surface in the troubled marriage and the breakup that may follow. The preceding chapters have examined a number of these. Similarly, there are typical responses and attitudes that may appear during the separation/divorce process and in the postdivorce period that characterize either a positive or negative adjustment to the dissolution of a marriage.

The studies cited earlier in this chapter highlighted some of the major inhibitors to positive adjustment for women who divorce. These include strong attachment to the ex-spouse, ongoing conflict with the ex-spouse, lack of social involvement, clinging to previous roles, resistance to accepting a work identity, and failure to explore new options. On the other hand, countless women have emerged from divorce to build new lives for themselves and their families. They have made a conscious decision to work through their loss and to move ahead with hope and new energy. In so doing, they have discovered within themselves new wellsprings of confidence, self-esteem, and competence.

The challenge for the divorced woman is to move beyond the trauma and disruption of marital breakup and focus on the future, with the firm conviction that she can be a whole person and can lead a full and healthy life. The following guidelines for rebuilding after divorce are gleaned from practical and clinical experience, as well as the advice of experts who have worked with divorced persons.

Accept the finality of divorce and the fact that the marriage has ended. It's normal to grieve and mourn the loss of the relationship, but the time comes to get on with your life. If you feel yourself becoming immobilized by depression, get professional help.

Express your anger, then move beyond it. Don't let feelings of anger, bitterness, regret and hurt dominate your life.

Work to establish a new identity for yourself, apart from your ex-spouse and your former roles in marriage. One woman who reluctantly divorced in mid-life reflected: "My marriage was an important part of my life, but it was not my whole life."

Invest in yourself. Learn to enjoy your new singleness. Emphasize your personal growth and work on building your self-confidence.

Detach emotionally from your ex-spouse. Resist the urge to "take care of him" as he struggles with his own adjustment problems.

Don't get caught in the morass of ongoing conflict with your ex-spouse over finances, children, and other issues. When communicating with him, try to handle the interaction in a businesslike way.

Be willing to venture into the unfamiliar and take new risks. This could include the work world, further education, new friendships, new hobbies, travel, and so on. It's a great way to rebuild confidence that may be shaken after the failure of a marriage.

Don't isolate yourself and withdraw from social contacts. Allowing yourself to become isolated and lonely can become a habit. It's also dangerous, as isolation can lead to overeating, drinking, and wallowing in self-pity.

Build new support networks. Reach out to family, friends, and co-workers and let them know you want their support and friendship.

Anticipate difficult times and plan ahead for ways to cope with them. Plan something special to do with other people on the day the divorce is finalized, on the anniversary of your marriage, on the day your ex-husband remarries.

Avoid situations that make you feel different and uncomfortable about being single. For example, before accepting social invitations, ask if you will be the only single person there. As one divorced woman advised, "Walk around the poison ivy, not into it."

Learn to take care of yourself—your body, your emotions, your spirit. Listen to your needs, value them, and find ways to meet them.

Take a proactive approach to planning your future. Believe you can survive and thrive!

The alternative to rebuilding your life after divorce is to stay caught in a time warp, stuck in the psychological and emotional space you occupied when your marriage failed. Few women would willingly choose to spend the rest of their lives there. But taking the first steps to rebuild may be difficult and painful. You may wonder, "How will I ever get beyond this?"

Many excellent resources are available in print on virtually all aspects of relationships, marriage, and divorce. You may find them helpful as you search for new insights and understanding, and as you begin the journey of rebuilding. We've included a few of these books in the appendix that follows. The list is by no means exhaustive, and your library and bookseller can provide others.

We can also learn much from other women who have taken steps to rebuild their lives after divorce and have sought out resources and strategies to aid and nourish them. What follows are the insights of some of these women, in their own words, about what helped them. (As with all the illustrations and case studies used in this book, the names of the women quoted below have been changed to preserve their privacy.) All of the women were divorced after several years of marriage; most had children at the time of separation. Their ages when they divorced ranged from thirty-one to forty-nine.

Sharon: "It was helpful to have friends that I could talk with at any time of the day or night. I knew they would keep my ramblings confidential, would not tire of my need to share my feelings, and would unconditionally listen. . . . It helped to have an attorney who was fair, honest, and completely there for me only. I would never recommend that husband and wife be represented by the same attorney. My attorney was very good at pointing out the ramifications of my own decisions and helping me to recognize my own needs after twenty-four years of always considering the needs of others first. . . . Taking time out for myself to exercise. This was important to my mental and physical health. . . . Being able to obtain good counseling on a regular basis. I firmly believe no one can go through such a loss without some professional counseling."

Molly: "I'd strongly recommend a support group for recently divorced/separated women. I needed to be with others who were still in the shock state and were still 'discovering,' just like me. It felt good to have solved a new problem or [to have] met a new challenge that I could share 'fresh' with someone who was facing the same dilemma. . . . I also found great solace in groups for singles that were faith-oriented. I needed (and need) to know that God did love me even if nobody else seemed to."

Connie: "Most of my sympathetic support came from strangers who later became friends. I went to a singles group connected with a church. The camaraderie of people in like circumstances or even worse circumstances helps to put your plight into perspective. . . . I found close relatives to not have any understanding of what I was going through. They thought only in financial terms, and as long as I could support myself they couldn't understand what my problem was. The distant relatives were much more supportive. . . . I found a female friend who had come from a similar economic background and was going through the approximate same steps of divorce at the same time. . . . I met and dated a man from the singles group—a relationship I should not have jumped into. I now wish I would have had more experience, time, and freedom to adjust to single life before getting involved with a very controlling man."

Norene: "I sought counseling with a qualified therapist. That enabled me to process my feelings and sort out what was important to me in a safe, nonjudgmental environment. . . . I talked at length to friends and family and gathered their support. I found that being open about my pain enabled other people to be open in their support of me. Having people who cared about me and who nurtured me made a big difference in maintaining my self-esteem. It also helped me to solve practical problems and to have people available to help me learn how to do things I had no experience with. I tried to be clear about how people could be of help to me and to let people know how much their support meant to me. . . . I learned what was truly important to me, what I needed and how to get it for myself. This proved to be the most important step in regaining a sense of myself as a separate person. That sense was vital to my self-esteem and to enabling me to move into the future. I found that the better I took care of myself the faster I was able to let go of the past and live in the present."

Betty: "I moved from our family home to a new home in order to try to let go of the memories that reminded me of life with my former husband. . . . I changed traditions, like inviting other people for dinner on special holidays that were once reserved for family only. . . . I learned to avoid situations that were painful for a divorced person, like being in church on Mother's Day when all the couples were asked to stand and hold hands. . . . I went into therapy to address unresolved issues to ensure that I wouldn't take old baggage into new relationships. . . . I prevented myself from living vicariously through my children. . . . I developed short- and long-term goals and a road map showing where I wanted to be in my career in ten years. . . .

I went to a financial planner who helped me develop a plan that will prevent me from feeling dependent upon others during retirement. . . . I learned to take better care of tasks. I didn't even know how to fill the tank of my car prior to our separation. . . . I have spent a great deal of time alone, and I have enjoyed my own company."

Margaret: "The important issue for me when my first husband and I separated was: What do I want? Not what my family, friends, or husband wanted, but what I wanted. . . . The next important job was sorting through my feelings of worth and individuality. Was I important enough to be a single woman in my own home, with my own job, life, and car? What could I respect about myself? Was I okay just by myself? Could I give up old notions of a traditional marriage and family, and then mourn their loss? Could I give up the idea of ever having children and a husband and still like myself? When I wrestled with these issues —with the help of a wonderful woman psychologist, as well as supportive family and friends—and realized I liked myself and could do OK alone, then my life was opened to all new possibilities and changes. Things were not always easy and many struggles ensued. . . . The grieving of a lost marriage was completed many years ago and now the hurt is gone. And, I believe a large reason was coming to grips with who I am and who I wanted to be and believing I was worth the effort—single or with a family; I could have lived happily either way. The self-esteem and love I had early in my life allowed these decisions to be made and issues to be resolved.

Kristin: "Probably the most helpful resource for me was my faith. I didn't blame God for all the pain and I didn't feel God was punishing me for being less than a perfect wife. My faith was a constant source of comfort. . . . Connecting with people was also healing. One can be tempted to recoil and isolate oneself. This is the time to reach out and ask friends to really be present for you. Every letter, every unexpected phone call from a friend or family member boosted my courage and self-esteem tremendously. . . . Books have become treasures to me. They helped me understand what I was—and wasn't—feeling. They prepared me for relating to my attorney, my former marriage partner, and my son. They removed a lot of my fears by providing me with the knowledge I needed to survive and meet each challenge. When I began to read, I began to reclaim my personal power. . . . I kept a journal, which takes a lot of discipline, but I learned so much about myself every time I would re-read a few entries. You can see the glimmers of new life and strength that are emerging. . . . Soft, gentle music and candlelight were gifts I gave myself, especially before bedtime. . . . I also took up some new hobbies like basketweaving, which allowed me to do something creative. . . . Therapy, of course, was invaluable. I gained insights about myself, my failed marriage, the dysfunctional patterns that contribute to many breakdowns, as well as ways to avoid the same pitfalls again."

Women can and do rebuild positive, new lives after divorce. They learn to draw on their own resources, find help and support when needed, and develop strategies for coping with the changes and difficulties they must face. Women who are beginning the process—or returning to it—can learn from the experiences of others who are willing to share the measures they took to find help, healing, and hope for a new life. The rebuilding process is not easy, and it is probably never completely finished. What is crucial, however, is that you begin the journey to recovery, that you keep it going, and that you don't look back.

NOTES

INTRODUCTION

1. Ann M. Morrison, Randall P. White, Ellen Van Velsor, and the Center for Creative Leadership, *Breaking the Glass Ceiling* (Massachusetts: Addison-Wesley, 1987).

2. Harriet G. Lerner, *The Dance of Anger* (New York: Harper & Row, 1985).

REFERENCES

Herbert Friedenberger, "Today's Troubled Men," *Psychology Today* (December 1987), pp. 46-47.

David Popenoe, "Family Decline in America," in David Blankenhorn, Steven Bayme, Jean Bethke Elshtain, eds., *Rebuilding the Nest: A New Commitment to the American Family* (Milwaukee: Family Service America, 1990), pp. 39-51.

CHAPTER 1

1. Edward M. Waring, *Enhancing Marital Intimacy Through Facilitating Cognitive Self-Disclosure* (New York: Brunner/Mazel, 1988).

2. Jim Sellner, Judy Sellner and Brenda Rabkin, "It's Always Something," *New Woman* (January 1990), p. 50.

3. Robert J. Sternberg, "A Triangular Theory of Love," *Psychological Review*, 93, pp. 119-135.

4. Ira D. Turkat and J.F. Calhoun, "The Problem-Solving Flowchart," *The Behavior Therapist* (1980), v. 3, no. 3, p. 21.

REFERENCES

Albert Ellis, *How to Stubbornly Refuse to Make Yourself Miserable About Anything—Yes, Anything!* (New Jersey: Lyle Stuart, 1988).

John Gray, *Men, Women and Relationships: Making Peace with the Opposite Sex* (Oregon: Beyond Words Publishing, Inc., 1990).

Harriet G. Lerner, *The Dance of Anger* (New York: Harper & Row, 1985).

CHAPTER 2

1. John Gray, *Men, Women and Relationships: Making Peace With the Opposite Sex* (Oregon: Beyond Words Publishing, Inc., 1990).

2. Art Levine, "The Second Time Around: Realities of Remarriage," *U.S. News and* World *Report* (January 29, 1990), pp. 50-51.

3. Deborah Tannen, *You Just Don't Understand: Women and Men in Conversation* (New York: Ballentine Books, a division of Random House, Inc., 1990).

4. Wayne E. Oates, "Therapeutic Deadlock in Impending Divorce Situations," in John F. Crosby (ed.), *When One Wants Out and the Other Doesn't: Doing Therapy with Polarized Couples* (New York: Brunner/Mazel, Inc., 1989), pp. 153-174.

5. John Gray, *Men, Women and Relationships.*

6. Harriet Goldhor Lerner, *The Dance of Intimacy* (New York: Harper and Row, 1989), p. 3.

7. Stephen R. Covey, *The Seven Habits of Highly Effective People: Powerful Lessons in Personal Change* (New York: Fireside/Simon and Schuster, 1989).

8. Paula McDonald and Dick McDonald, "Freedom Is . . . . ," excerpted from *Loving Free* (New York: Ballantine, 1973).

REFERENCES

Leo Buscaglia, *Loving Each Other: The Challenge of Human Relationships* (New Jersey: Slack Incorporated, 1984).

Stanley R. Graham, "What Does a Man Want?" *American Psychologist* (July 1992), pp. 837-941.

John Gray, *Men Are From Mars, Women Are From Venus: A Practical Guide For Improving Communication and Getting What You Want in Your Relationships* (New York: Harper Collins, 1992).

Neil S. Jacobson, Ph.D., "Working With Difficult Couples—Integrating Acceptance and Change: A Cognitive Perspective." A presentation at the Milwaukee Psychiatric Hospital, Milwaukee, Wisconsin, July 16, 1992.

Anne Wilson Schaef, *Escape From Intimacy: The Pseudo-Relationship Addictions* (San Francisco: Harper and Row, 1989).

Brenda Schaeffer, *Is It Love, Or Is It Addiction?* (New York: Harper Collins, 1989).

Anestasia Toufexis, "The Right Chemistry: Evolutionary Roots, Brain Imprints, Biological Secretions. That's the Story of Love," *Time* (February 15, 1993) pp. 49-51.

Judith S. Wallerstein and Sandra Blakeslee, *Second Chances: Men, Women, and Children a Decade After Divorce* (New York: Ticknor & Fields, 1990).

CHAPTER 3

1. Martha Haffey & Phyllis Malkin Cohen, "Treatment Issues for Divorcing Women," *Families in Society* (March 1992), pp. 142-148.

2. Laura Jereski, "Managing a Divorce Like a Business," *Working Woman* (Feb. 1993), p. 30.

3. Lenore J. Weitzman, *The Divorce Revolution: the Unexpected Social and Economic Consequences for Women and Children in America* (New York: Free Press, 1985).

4. Saul D. Hoffman & Greg J. Duncan, "What Are the Economic Consequences of Divorce?" *Demography* (Nov. 1988), p. 641.

5. Richard R. Peterson, *Women, Work, and Divorce* (Albany: State University of New York Press, 1989).

6. Susan Moller Okin, "Economic Equality After Divorce," *Dissent* (Summer 1991), pp. 383-387.

CHAPTER 4

1. Sharron K. St. John (Pastoral Counseling Services of Milwaukee, Wisconsin), "On Deserving To Feel Good," *Network, the Newsletter of United Church of Christ Women in Wisconsin,* (January 1990).

2. *Women and Depression: Risk Factors and Treatment Issues.* The final report of the American Psychological Association's National Task Force on Women and Depression (Washington, D. C. : American Psychological Association, May 1991).

3. Robert M. A. Hirschfeld and C. K. Cross, "Epidemiology of Affective Disorders: Psychosocial Risk Factors," *Archives of General Psychiatry* 39, (1982): 35-46.

4. John H. Greist and James W. Jefferson, *Depression and its Treatment: Help for the Nation's #1 Mental Problem* (Washington, D. C. : American Psychiatric Press, Inc., 1984).

5. E. S. Shneidman, *Definition of Suicide* (New York: Wiley, 1985).

6. American Psychiatric Association, *Diagnostic and Statistical Manual of Mental Disorders* (4th ed.), (Washington, D. C. : American Psychiatric Association, 1994).

7. Brana Lobel and Robert M. A. Hirschfeld, *Depression: What We Know* (Maryland: U.S. Department of Health and Human Services, NIMH contract number 102236553, 1984).

8. Dennis P. Cantwell, M.D., and Jack A. Morgenstern, M.D., "Attention Deficit Hyperactivity Disorders." Key presenters at the ADHD conference at the University of Minnesota, November 5, 1990.

9. Carol Tavris and Carole Offir, *The Longest War: Sex Differences in Perspective* (New York: Harcourt Brace Jovanovich, Inc., 1977), p. 190.

10. John Naisbitt, *Megatrends* (New York: Warner Books, 1984).

11. Marilyn Sargent, *Depressive Disorders: Treatments Bring New Hope* (Maryland: U.S. Department of Health and Human Services, 1986).

12. "Antidepressants Update," Talk Paper, a summary of the FDA's Psychopharmacological Drugs Advisory Committee meeting of September 20, 1991, and issued by the Food and Drug Administration, U.S. Department of Health and Human Services, Public Health Service. No. T91-64, October 18, 1991.

13. Philip Elmer-Dewitt, "Depression: The Growing Role of Drug Therapies," *Time* (July 6, 1992), pp. 57-60.

14. Albert Ellis, "Rational-emotive Therapy," in Raymond J. Corsini and Danny Wedding (eds.) *Current Psychotherapies* (4th ed.) (Illinois: F.E. Peacock Publishers, Inc., 1989), pp. 197-238.

15. J. Raymond DePaulo, Jr. and Keith Russell Ablow, *How To Cope With Depression: A Complete Guide for You and Your Family* (New York: McGraw Hill Publishing Company, 1989).

16. American Psychiatric Association, *Diagnostic and Statistical Manual of Mental Disorders* (4th ed.).

REFERENCES

Aaron T. Beck and Marjorie E. Weishaar, "Cognitive Therapy," in Raymond J. Corsini and Danny Wedding (eds.) *Current Psychotherapies* (4th ed.) (Illinois: F.E. Peacock Publishers, Inc., 1989), pp. 285-320.

Gerald Corey, *Theory and Practice of Counseling and Psychotherapy* (4th ed.) (Pacific Grove, California: Brooks/Cole Publishing Company, 1991).

Gerald Corey and Marianne Schneider Corey, *Groups: Process and Practice* (California: Wadsworth Publishing Company, Inc., 1977).

Charles J. Gelso and Bruce R. Fretz, *Counseling Psychology* (Fort Worth: Harcourt Brace Jovanovich College Publishers, 1992).

John Gray, *Men, Women and Relationships: Making Peace With the Opposite Sex* (Oregon: Beyond Words Publishing, Inc., 1990).

Herbert Hendin, *Suicide in America* (New York: W.W. Norton and Company, Inc., 1982).

The ADD Hyperactivity Handbook for Schools (Florida: Impact Publications, Inc., 1992).

CHAPTER 5

1. Rosalind D. Cartwright, "Dreams That Work: The Relations of Dream Incorporation to Adaptation to Stressful Events," *Journal of the Association for the Study of Dreams* (1991), v. 1, pp. 3-9.

2. Elisabeth Kubler-Ross, *On Death and Dying* (New York: Macmillan, 1969).

3. Barry Lubetkin and Elena Oumano, *Bailing Out: The Healthy Way to Get Out of a Bad Relationship and Survive* (New York: Simon and Schuster, Inc., 1991).

4. *The Sacred Tree*, produced by Judie Bopp, Michael Bopp, Lee Brown and Phil Lane for The Four Worlds Development Project, The University of Lethbridge (Alberta: The Four Worlds Development Press, 1985), p. 56.

5. *Random Acts of Kindness*, by the editors of Conari Press, 1993, p. 56.

REFERENCES

John Bradshaw, "How Resentment Can Wreck Divorce," *Lears* (August, 1990), p. 57.

Stephen R. Covey, *The Seven Habits of Highly Effective People: Powerful Lessons in Personal Change* (New York: Fireside/Simon and Schuster, 1989).

Bruce Fisher, *Rebuilding: When Your Relationship Ends* (California: Impact Publishers, 1987).

Bertha G. Simos, *A Time to Grieve: Loss as a Universal Human Experience* (New York: Family Service Association of America, 1979).

CHAPTER 6

1. Christopher F. Clulow, "Divorce as Bereavement: Similarities and Differences," *Family and Conciliation Courts Review* (June 1990), pp. 19-22.

2. Judith S. Wallerstein and Sandra Blakeslee, *Second Chances: Men, Women, and Children a Decade After Divorce* (New York: Ticknor & Fields, 1989), p. 13.

3. Judith S. Wallerstein and Joan Berlin Kelly, *Surviving the Breakup: How Children and Parents Cope With Divorce* (New York: Basic Books, Inc., 1980), pp. 35-36.

4. E. Mavis Hetherington, "Long-Term Effects of Divorce and Remarriage on the Adjustment of Children," *Journal of the American Academy of Child Psychiatry* (Sept. 1985), pp 518-530.

5. Richard A. Warshak, The Custody Revolution: *The Father Factor and the Motherhood Mystique* (New York: Poseidon Press, 1992).

6. Andrew J. Cherlin, F.F. Furstenberg Jr., P.L. Chase-Lansdale, K.E. Kiernan, P.K. Robins, D.R. Morrison, J.O. Teitler, "Longitudinal Studies of Effects of Divorce on Children in Great Britain and the United States," *Science* (June 1991), pp. 1386-1389.

7. Frank J. Furstenberg, Jr. and Andrew J. Cherlin, *Divided Families: What Happens to Children When Parents Part* (Cambridge: Harvard University Press, 1991), p. 68.

8. Wallerstein and Kelly, p. 39.

9. Wallerstein and Blakeslee, p. 11.

10. Ibid., p. 15.

11. Wallerstein and Kelly, p. 17.

12. Ibid., p. 46.

13. John W. Santrock and Russel L. Tracy, "Effects of Children's Family Structure on the Development of Stereotypes by Teachers," *Journal of Educational Psychology* (Oct. 1978), pp. 754-757.

14. James L. Peterson and Nicholas Zill, "Marital Disruption, Parent-Child Relationships, and Behavior Problems in Children," *Journal of Marriage and the Family* (May 1986), pp. 295-307.

15. Wallerstein and Kelly, pp. 10-11.

16. Richard A. Gardner, M.D., *The Parents Book About Divorce* (New York: Bantam Books, 1991), p. 54.

17. Wallerstein and Kelly, p. 207.

REFERENCES

Frank F. Furstenberg, Jr., "Divorce and the American Family," *Annual Review of Sociology* (Palo Alto: Annual Reviews Inc., vol. 16, 1990).

Judith S. Wallerstein, "The Long-Term Effects of Divorce on Children: A Review," *Journal of the American Academy of Child and Adolescent Psychiatry* (May 1991).

CHAPTER 7

1. Martha Haffey and Phyllis Malkin Cohen, "Treatment Issues for Divorcing Women," *Families in Society* (March 1992), pp. 142-148.

2. Ibid.

3. Ellen B. Bogolub, "Women and Mid-life Divorce: Some Practice Issues," *Social Work* (Sept. 1991), pp. 428-433.

4. Judith S. Wallerstein and Sandra Blakeslee, *Second Chances: Men, Women and Children a Decade After Divorce* (New York: Ticknor & Fields, 1989).

5. Ibid.

6. Gay C. Kitson, *Portrait of Divorce* (New York: The Guilford Press, 1992), p. 20.

7. Ibid.

8. Jeanne M. Tschann, Janet R. Johnston and Judith S. Wallerstein, "Resources, Stressors, and Attachment as Predictors of Adult Adjustment After Divorce: a Longitudinal Study," *Journal of Marriage and the Family* (Nov. 1989), pp. 1033-1046.

9. Marion H. Wijnbeerg and Thomas Holmes, "Adaptation to Divorce: the Impact of Role Orientation on Family-life-cycle Perspectives," *Families in Society* (March 1992), pp. 159-167.

10. Ibid.

11. Nancy Paul and Andrea Warfield, "The Impact of Divorce on Work," *Personnel Management* (Feb. 1990), pp. 28-31.

12. Toni L'Hommedieu, *The Divorce Experience of Working and Middle Class Women* (Ann Arbor: UMI Research Press, 1984).

13. Krisanne Bursik, "Adaptation to Divorce and Ego Development in Adult Women," *Journal of Personality and Social Psychology* (Feb. 1991), pp. 300-306.

14. Wallerstein and Blakeslee, p. 30.

ABOUT THE AUTHORS

Beverly J. Grottkau, Ph.D., is a psychotherapist, adult educator, and author. Her work has been published in professional journals, including *Educational Research Quarterly, Education, Journal of Lifelong Learning,* and *Journal of the National Association of Women Deans, Administrators and Counselors.*

She has served on the faculties of Concordia University Wisconsin, Carthage College, and the University of Wisconsin-Milwaukee. She has designed, developed, and implemented training programs for adult students in the areas of health care, counseling, human relations, and education and has made presentations and conducted workshops at conferences and seminars throughout the United States and Europe.

Dr. Grottkau was Director of the International Training Center of Family Service America, an association of 300 family service agencies in the United States and Canada. She is currently a psychotherapist in private practice, specializing in the treatment of women with a variety of presenting disorders. She also works extensively with couples in various stages of marital conflict and frequently makes presentations to women and men who are contemplating divorce or who have finalized divorce proceedings.

Dr. Grottkau completed her undergraduate work at the University of Iowa and earned a Master's degree and Ph.D. from the University of Wisconsin-Milwaukee. She has completed a postgraduate course of study at the C. G. Jung Institute in Zurich, Switzerland. She has received grants for projects in community service and for work with high-risk youth. She was the recipient of the Milwaukee Council for Adult Learning Annual Distinguished Service Award for outstanding leadership in adult education.

Dr. Grottkau was appointed by the Chief Justice of the State of Wisconsin Supreme Court to the Equal Justice Task Force, a 28-member group charged to investigate the extent to which gender impacts the delivery of legal services and the opportunities for fair and accessible treatment in the legal system, and to make recommendations for methods of eliminating gender-related problems identified through that investigation.

Eva Augustin Rumpf, M.A. is a free-lance journalist who has been published in dozens of national and regional magazines and newspapers. Ms. Rumpf worked for several years as a reporter for *The Milwaukee Journal*, a major daily newspaper serving Wisconsin. She served on the staff of the former mayor of Milwaukee, Henry W. Maier, and has also worked as a public relations and marketing professional for a number of organizations, including Family Service America, and has operated her own consulting business. She has developed scores of newsletters, brochures, annual reports, news releases, scripts, speeches, and promotional materials for businesses and organizations. Ms. Rumpf has received awards for her writing from the International Association of Business Communicators, the Milwaukee Ad Club, and the Wisconsin Hospital Public Relations Council

Ms. Rumpf's broad experience has enabled her to develop journalistic expertise in a wide range of areas, including family and parenting issues, education, health care, fitness, business, and social concerns. She has conducted communications workshops around the country and previously taught journalism at

Marquette University in Milwaukee. Ms. Rumpf currently serves as Student Publications Director and journalism instructor at Texas Christian University in Fort Worth, Texas.

Ms. Rumpf received a Bachelor of Arts degree in English from Elmhurst College, Elmhurst, Illinois, and a Master of Arts degree in journalism from Marquette University.

BIBLIOGRAPHY

Further Reading for Adults

THE DIVORCE PROCESS

Ahrons, Constance. *The Good Divorce* (New York: Harper Collins, 1994).

Everett, Craig and Sandra Volgy Everett. *Healthy Divorce* (San Francisco: Jossey-Bass, 1994).

Gold, Lois. *Between Love and Hate: A Guide to Civilized Divorce* (New York: Plenum Press, 1992).

Kressel, Kenneth. *The Process of Divorce* (New York: Basic Books, Inc., 1985).

Neumann, Diane. *Divorce Mediation: How to Cut the Cost and Stress of Divorce* (New York: Henry Holt & Co., 1989).

Robertson, Christina. *A Woman's Guide to Divorce and Decision Making* (New York: Fireside, 1989).

Rogers, Mary. *Women, Divorce and Money* (New York: McGraw-Hill, 1981).

Ware, Ciji. *Sharing Parenthood After Divorce: An Enlightened Custody Guide for Mothers, Fathers, and Kids* (New York: The Viking Press, 1982).

Wheeler, Michael. *Divided Children: A Legal Guide for Divorcing Parents* (New York: William Norton & Co., 1980).

RELATIONSHIPS

Beattie, Melody. *Codependent No More: How to Stop Controlling Others and Start Caring For Yourself* (New York: HarperCollins Publishers, 1987).

Crabb, Larry. *Men and Women: Enjoying the Difference* (Michigan: Zondervan Publishing House, 1991).

Fowler, Richard and Rita Schwartz. *Together on a Tightrope* (Tennessee: Thomas Nelson, Inc., 1991).

Gray, John. *Men Are From Mars, Women Are From Venus: A Practical Guide For Improving Communication and Getting What You Want in Your Relationships* (New York: HarperCollins, 1992).

Gray, John. *Men, Women and Relationships: Making Peace With the Opposite Sex* (Oregon: Beyond Words Publishing, Inc. 1990).

Whitfield, Charles L. *Boundaries and Relationships: Knowing, Protecting and Enjoying the Self* (Florida: Health Communications, Inc., 1993).

Wilson, Sandra D. *Hurt People Hurt People: Hope and Healing For Yourself and Your Relationships* (Tennessee: Thomas Nelson, Inc., 1993).

HANDLING YOUR FEELINGS

Beattie, Melody. *The Language of Letting Go: Daily Meditations For Codependents* (New York: HarperCollins Publishers, 1990).

Bradshaw, John. *Healing the Shame that Binds You* (Florida: Health Communications, Inc., 1988).

Branden, Nathaniel. *How to Raise Your Self-esteem* (New York: Doubleday Dell Publishing, 1987).

Briggs, Dorothy Corkille. *Celebrate Your Self: Enhancing Your Self-esteem* (New York: Doubleday Dell Publishing, 1977).

Burns, David. *Feeling Good: The New Mood Therapy* (New York: William Morrow & Co., 1980).

Buscaglia, Leo, *Personhood: The Art of Being Fully Human* (New York: Fawcett Columbine, 1978).

DePaulo, J. Raymond, Jr., and Keith Russell Ablow. *How To Cope With Depression: A Complete Guide For You and Your Family* (New York: McGraw Hill Publishing Company, 1989).

Ellis, Albert. *How To Stubbornly Refuse to Make Yourself Miserable About Anything—Yes, Anything!* (New Jersey: Lyle Stuart, 1988).

Lerner, Harriet Goldhor. *The Dance of Deception* (New York: Harper and Row, 1993).

Lerner, Harriet Goldhor. *The Dance of Intimacy* (New York: Harper and Row, 1989).

Lerner, Harriet Goldhor. *The Dance of Anger* (New York: Harper and Row, 1985).

Tavris, Carol. *Anger: The Misunderstood Emotion* (New York: Simon and Schuster, 1989).

Treadwell, Perry. *Making Friends: Leaving Loneliness Behind* (Florida: Health Communications, Inc., 1993).

HELPING CHILDREN COPE

Anderson, Jill. *Thinking, Changing, Rearranging: Improving Self-esteem in Young People* (Oregon: Timerbline Press, Inc., 1981).

Furstenberg, Frank F., Jr., and Andrew J. Cherlin. *Divided Families: What Happens to Children When Parents Part* (Cambridge: Harvard University Press, 1991).

Gardner, Richard A. *The Parents Book about Divorce* (New York: Doubleday, 1991).

Gordon, Thomas. *P.E.T. Parent Effectiveness Training* (New York: Penguin Books, 1975).

Teyber, Edward. *Helping Children Cope in Divorce* (New York: Lexington Books, 1992).

REBUILDING AFTER DIVORCE

Bell, Terry, and Steve Joiner. *Common Sense Recovery: Dealing With Divorce* (Texas: Abilene Christian University Press, 1990).

Bolles, Richard Nelson. *What Color is Your Parachute?* (Berkeley: Ten Speed Press, 1993).

Brandt, Patricia with Dave Jackson. *A Course for Single Parents* (Illinois: David C. Cook Publishing Company, 1985).

Colgrove, Melba, Harold H. Bloomfield, and Peter McWilliams. *How To Survive the Loss of a Love* (California: Prelude Press, 1991).

English, Martin. *How to Feel Great About Yourself and Your Life* (New York: Amacom, 1992).

Fisher, Bruce. *Rebuilding: When Your Relationship Ends* (California: Impact Publishers, 2nd edition, 1992).

Krantzler, Melvin. *Creative Divorce: A New Opportunity for Personal Growth* (New York: M. Evans & Co., 1978).

Lubetkin, Barry, and Elena Oumano. *Bailing Out: The Healthy Way to Get Out of a Bad Relationship and Survive* (New York: Simon and Schuster, Inc., 1991).

Peck, M. Scott. *The Road Less Traveled* (New York: Simon and Schuster, 1978).

Robertson, John, and Betty Utterback. *Suddenly Single: Learning to Start Over Through the Experience of Others* (New York: Simon and Schuster, 1986).

Sills, Judith. *Excess Baggage: Getting Out of Your Own Way* (New York: Viking, 1993).

Singleton, Mary Ann. *Life After Marriage* (New York: Stein and Day, 1974).

Wilkie, Jane. *The Divorced Woman's Handbook: An Outline for Starting the First Year Alone* (New York: William Morrow & Co., 1980).

Williamson, Marianne. *A Return To Love: Reflections on the Principles of a Course in Miracles* (New York: HarperCollins Publishers, 1992).

Young, Jeffrey E., and Janet S. Klako. *Reinventing Your Life: How To Break Free From Negative Life Patterns* (New York: Dutton, 1993).

Books for Children and Teens

BOOKS FOR YOUNG CHILDREN

Brown, Laurene Krasny, and Marc Brown. *Dinosaurs Divorce: A Guide for Changing Families* (Boston: Joy Street Books, Little Brown and Co., 1986).

Caines, Jeannette. *Daddy* (New York: Harper and Row, 1977).

Dragonwagon, Crescent. *Always, Always* (New York: Macmillan, 1984).

Paris, Lena. *Mom Is Single* (Chicago: Children's Press, 1980).

Perry, Patricia, and Marietta Lynch. *Mommy and Daddy Are Divorced* (New York: Dial Books for Young Readers, 1978).

Schuchman, Joan. *Two Places to Sleep* (Minneapolis: Carolrhoda Books, 1979).

Thomas, Ianthe. *Eliza's Daddy* (New York: Harcourt Brace Jovanovich, 1976).

Vigna, Judith. *She's Not My Real Mother* (Chicago: Albert Whitman and Co., 1980).

FICTION FOR OLDER CHILDREN AND TEENS

Blume, Judy. *It's Not the End of the World* (Scarsdale, N.Y.: Bradbury Press, 1972).

Cleary, Beverly. *Dear Mr. Henshaw* (New York: William Morrow & Co., 1983).

Danziger, Paula. *The Pistachio Prescription* (New York: Dell, 1978).

Hurwitz, Johanna. *DeDe Takes Charge* (New York: William Morrow & Co., 1984).

Mann, Peggy. *My Dad Lives in A Downtown Hotel* (Garden City, N.Y.: Doubleday & Co., Inc., 1973).

Mazer, Norma Fox. *Taking Terri Mueller* (New York: William Morrow & Co., 1981).

NONFICTION FOR OLDER CHILDREN AND TEENS

Dolmetsch, Paul, and Alexa Sheh (ed.). *The Kids' Book About Single-Parent Families* (Garden City, N.Y.: Doubleday and Co., 1985). (Written by children ages 11-15.)

Gardner, Richard A. *The Boys and Girls Book About Divorce* (New York: Bantam Books, 1970).

Krementz, Jill. *How It Feels When Parents Divorce* (New York: Alfred A. Knopf, 1984). (Children ages 7-16 share their feelings about divorce.)

Le Shan, Eda. *What's Going to Happen to Me? When Parents Separate or Divorce* (New York: Four Winds Press, 1978).

Richards, Arlene, and Irene Willis. *How to Get it Together When Your Parents Are Coming Apart* (New York: David McKay Co., 1976).

The Unit at Fayerweather Street School, Eric E. Rofes, editor. *The Kids' Book of Divorce* (Lexington, Mass.: The Lewis Publishing Co., 1981). (Written by children ages 11-14.)

INDEX

225